THE INTERNATIONAL BUSINESSWOMAN OF THE 1990s

THE INTERNATIONAL BUSINESSWOMAN OF THE 1990s

A Guide to Success in the Global Marketplace

Marlene L. Rossman

PRAEGER

New York
Westport, Connecticut
London

Library of Congress Cataloging-in-Publication Data

Rossman, Marlene L.
　　The international businesswoman of the 1990s : a guide to success in the global marketplace / Marlene L. Rossman.
　　　　p.　　cm.
　　Rev. ed. of: The international businesswoman. 1986.
　　Includes bibliographical references.
　　ISBN 0-275-93329-6 (alk. paper)
　　1. Women executives.　2. Women in business.　3. Negotiation in business.　　I. Rossman, Marlene L.　International businesswoman.　II. Title.
HD6054.3.R67　　　1990
650.1'024042—dc20　　　　　89-70950

Copyright © 1990 by Marlene L. Rossman

All rights reserved. No portion of this book may be reproduced, by any process or technique, without the express written consent of the publisher.

Library of Congress Catalog Card Number: 89-70950
ISBN: 0-275-93329-6

First published in 1990

Praeger Publishers, One Madison Avenue, New York, NY 10010
An imprint of Greenwood Publishing Group, Inc.

Printed in the United States of America

The paper used in this book complies with the Permanent Paper Standard issued by the National Information Standards Organization (Z39.48-1984).

10　9　8　7　6　5　4　3　2　1

Contents

Preface
ix

Introduction
xi

1

Women in Business: A World of Opportunity
1

2

Preparing for Your Career
in International Business
13

3

Careers in International Business
23

4

Doing Business in the World Marketplace:
An Introduction to International Negotiating
33

5
Doing Business in the World Marketplace:
Asia, the Far East, and Down Under
53

6
Doing Business in the World Marketplace:
Europe 1992 and Beyond
65

7
Doing Business in the World Marketplace:
Latin America
75

8
Doing Business in the World Marketplace:
Africa and the Middle East
85

9
Doing Business in the World Marketplace:
The United States and Canada
95

10
The International Businesswoman at Home:
Working in the United States for a Foreign Firm
105

11
Breaking Down Barriers: Nine Stories
111

12
Global Marketing
125

13
Your Power Presence
133

14

Life on the Road: Traveling for Business
143

15

Career, Love, and Family: Having It All
157

16

Women in the World Marketplace: 2000 A.D.
167

Bibliography
171

Preface

I first wrote *The International Businesswoman* for professional and university women who were intrigued and excited by the world of international business and wanted to learn more about opportunities open to them. In the four years since the first book came out, there has been an explosion not only in global business, but also in the opportunities for women in this expanding field.

In the last decade, we have seen a growing number of U.S. firms acquired by or merged with foreign companies, blurring the distinction between domestic and international business. International business is no longer conducted only in New York and Los Angeles, but in every city and town across the United States. We are seeing Western Europe unite, and Eastern Europe open up to new economic progress. With new computer and communications technology, you can do business with four continents without leaving your office—or your home.

As we are moving closer to the global economy of the twenty-first century, the opportunities for women are growing and changing. Women are no longer fighting for bit parts in a male-directed play; global business requires new management philosophies based on cooperation and teamwork, rather than on cutthroat competition.

Women, whose upbringing has traditionally emphasized these skills, are becoming the new stars on the global stage.

This new edition will guide you through the rapidly changing landscape. I examine the opportunities—and the pitfalls—in such new global arrangements as the U.S.–Canada trade pact, the unification of the European Economic Community, and the spread of *perestroika* through the Eastern bloc. I also explore the new opportunities for women in business ranging from family-owned companies to global conglomerates. This book will tell you how to cope if your company is acquired by the Japanese, if you're sent on a business trip to Zurich, or if your Argentinian client comes to visit your office in Indianapolis.

In 1984, I was asked to speak about my career to the Women's Career Forum at New York University's Graduate School of Business. The women overwhelmed me with questions about how they could prepare for a career in international business. I found that although there were a number of books about doing business overseas, none dealt specifically with women entering this field. These women were asking the same questions that I had faced when I first entered this formerly all-male preserve.

As I did research for my first book, I listed the qualities that make for a successful international negotiator. I realized that the flexibility, patience, and tolerance that characterize so many women are precisely the qualities so desperately needed in the international arena. As I researched the new developments in the field for this second edition, I found that I was not the only one to have this insight. Many corporations are beginning to recognize that women can be a secret weapon in the trade wars, and have been sending them, in increasing numbers, to the front lines. This book will give you the ammunition you need if your company drafts you for a mission to Tokyo, London, or Mexico City.

You don't have to travel overseas to use this book, however. International business is being conducted every day here in the United States. In fact, in this new edition, I've included a chapter on working in the United States for a foreign firm. Wherever you are, if you have the skill, knowledge, and determination, you'll find a world of opportunity waiting for you!

I'd like to thank a few people whose assistance and encouragement helped me write this book: the staff of Praeger Publishers, especially my editor, Alison Bricken; Felicia Morales, who helped with the manuscript; and my husband, Elliot Silverman, without whom there wouldn't have been a book.

Introduction

The world is shrinking in every sense—not only in communications and transportation (consider the Concorde, satellite and data networks, and the now-ubiquitous fax machine), but commercially as well. Global advertising, marketing, planning, trading, manufacturing, and joint ventures are not just buzzwords, but operating realities.

Since so much business is international in scope, we have learned that the only way to do volume business in the international market is to get out of U.S. headquarters and get on the road. As many women are traveling within the United States and gaining acceptance as a result of their drive, competence, and perseverance, the same things are beginning to happen in the international arena.

In 1988, Americans took more than 155 million business trips. A large group of Americans are also working for multinational corporations or are on long-term assignment for their company. In the past few years, women have begun to enter the international market in more than just token numbers.

The growth in international trade and travel is only one side of the story, however. There are still deep-seated cultural differences between the United States and other countries. A business traveler to Chicago, Riyadh, Buenos Aires, or Milan may see the same Coca-Cola or Toyota signs in the airport in each city, but she will be mistaken if she thinks the business culture in each location will be alike.

While negotiating sales and contracts in the United States is not an easy task, conducting business is a good deal more difficult in the international marketplace. Misinterpreted signals, missed cues, overt errors, small slights, and a host of unknowns can foul a deal. Not only can millions of dollars be forfeited, but future opportunities in a market can be destroyed forever. If a deal is lost because a businesswoman doesn't know the cultural norms, you can be sure that her company will never get another chance. Foreign executives are often a tightly knit social group, bound together by strong interpersonal relationships. A businesswoman who unknowingly breaks a social taboo may find other doors in the same locale permanently closed. On the other hand, businesswomen who take the time to become attuned to cultural considerations can negotiate contracts, make sales, and more important, open entire markets for their companies.

The key to doing business overseas is to be well prepared. First, you must arm yourself with extensive "hard skills," develop a confident personality, and gain expertise in the product or service you are selling. Second, speaking the language of the country in which you are working is a great advantage. Fluency, although a big plus, is not necessary, but knowing even a few words can make a difference. Political sophistication and knowing what *not* to say is often even more critical. Third, and most important, is learning the business culture. While business practices are different throughout the world, in most places overseas you must spend long hours getting to know your customer. In Latin America, the Middle East, and Asia especially, be prepared to have a few "getting acquainted" meetings before getting down to business. You may feel you're drinking enough coffee or tea to float home, but that's the way business is done. In those areas of the world, a relationship of trust must be established first, or your proposals will not be taken seriously.

What about doing business in countries not known for their liberal attitudes toward women? There are still some unspoken barriers to entry, but for the most part, a U.S. businesswoman, properly prepared, can succeed anywhere. Western Europe and Latin America are more open to women than some other regions; moreover, the U.S. businesswoman in many countries often is perceived as a U.S. businessperson. You must do whatever you can to foster that image. A firm handshake and knowing how to present yourself go far to break down resistance. Always keep your sense of humor, and think of how long it took the United States to accept women executives. As a woman, you probably couldn't have held your current position 20 years ago in the United States, so be patient with men in parts of the world who have rarely or never done business with a woman.

What about nonbusiness hours? The same rules apply as when doing business domestically. Try, if possible, to keep your business acquaintances just that. Romance and business do not mix well anywhere in the world. That doesn't mean you must sit in your hotel room during your entire stay. There are many ways to meet interesting people overseas without mixing fun and work. Good bets are religious, trade, and university affiliations where you can notify members in advance of your arrival. There is nothing like being welcomed into a home or club in a place 7,500 miles from home!

Increasingly, women are being presented with opportunities for business travel, long-term assignments, relocation overseas, and management positions in the United States with foreign-owned corporations. While overseas long-term assignments used to be a place to dump managers or derail them from the fast track, nowadays quite the opposite is true. Long- and short-term overseas experience gives you a tremendous edge when back in the United States. While the world may be shrinking, your professional horizons will be expanding.

THE INTERNATIONAL BUSINESSWOMAN OF THE 1990s

1

Women in Business: A World of Opportunity

In this shrinking world, business is becoming global in scope, making new opportunities appear in many industries. In the past, women were often excluded from most significant business opportunities. There are those who argue that we still are. In 1988, women on average earned about 70 cents for each dollar paid to men. Battles are raging in the courts over comparable worth, the argument that jobs traditionally dominated by women should be paid equally to occupations traditionally held by men. But for women who make it into the corporate world, the opportunities are unbounded.

As the year 2000 approaches, gains for women are coming in every traditional male bastion. Women are entering law, medicine, business, and engineering in huge numbers. Women make up approximately 54 percent of the U.S. work force, and 50 percent of the professional work force—almost 50 million women. In 1986 women represented almost 20 percent of lawyers, over 17 percent of doctors, over 44 percent of accountants, and over 36 percent of executives, managers, and administrators. Additionally, women are opening their own businesses in record numbers. Companies owned by women now account for close to 50 billion dollars in sales. Women own more than 4 million of the 13 million small U.S. businesses, and are the fastest growing entrepreneurial segment. This is a tremendous change from even ten years ago. Twenty years ago women didn't have more than a token representation in most occupations.

Gains are being made not only by white women, but by black, Asian, and other minority women as well. The Equal Employment Opportunity Commission has reported that in 1984 there were 75,000 black female officials and managers in U.S. businesses—three times the number there were ten years earlier.

A number of significant factors have led to growing participation and mobility in the workplace. One of the first major forces was the Civil Rights Movement of the late 1950s and 1960s, which galvanized women into an awareness of the inequalities of our society. The publication of Betty Friedan's *Feminine Mystique* applied these issues directly to the role of women. The popularity of the birth control pill in the 1960s led to a sexual revolution. Almost overnight, long-standing sexual taboos were thrown out. The 1960s was an era of protest. The Vietnam War was the first war in our country's history to be bitterly resisted by millions of people. At the same time, middle-class boys and girls began to experiment with hard and soft drugs in an unprecedented fashion. The estimated 75 million baby boomers, who started to come of age in a society that was radically different from that of the late 1940s to late 1950s of their childhood, were also prepared to face changes in other aspects of society, including the role of women. Additionally, the recession of the early 1970s forced women into the workplace in the largest numbers since World War II.

Young women, accustomed to protest and encouraged by the loosening of traditional mores, began to demand equality. After a militant phase, through which all protest movements pass, a quiet revolution began to take shape. Education became the greatest equalizer of all.

Women still have quite a way to go, as shown by a recent survey of graduating MBAs, who reported that men's attitudes toward women in management are as negative as the year before. But over the longer term, however, attitudes are improving. In a survey of 348 male executives conducted in 1985 by two Baylor University researchers, 47 percent said they would feel comfortable working for a woman, up from 27 percent in a similar study conducted in 1965. Moreover, in a 1989 survey of 1,500 readers of the *Wall Street Journal* (88 percent of them male), 79 percent of the men (and 82 percent of the women) said they wouldn't object to working for a woman. Thus, through incremental changes in the business and political climate, the gains that we have made will hopefully continue to increase.

There were a few women who had successful careers even before the women's movement of the 1970s. But these "queen bees" were considered oddities in the repressive society of the 1950s and early 1960s. Even in 1965 I was discouraged from taking business courses, although I went to a predominately business-oriented college.

Until recently, many women who worked felt guilty about doing so. As a result, they tended to overcompensate. They often held two full-time jobs, their career and that of wife and mother. One woman told me of constantly having to justify her profession to the likes of the PTA and Cub Scouts. While these women had supportive husbands, they felt they had to do all the housework themselves. And when they were at work, they often felt they had to be totally on guard with their male colleagues. One woman said she was always afraid of doing something a man wouldn't do, like leaving early to go watch her child be an onion in a school play. Even today, many women executives still feel more comfortable saying they are leaving early to meet with their accountant than saying they need to accompany their child to an interview with the admissions director of a summer computer camp.

These early professional pioneers often took sabbaticals in their careers to have children. The majority of today's professional women rarely fall off the fast track even if they do have children. Many women return to their jobs after a short leave. Women today often postpone motherhood until they have established themselves in their careers. They are waiting until well past age 30 to have their first child, a phenomenon virtually unheard of 20 years ago. Men are becoming much more actively involved in the parenting of children and in the general maintenance of the home.

Many women have found new ways of balancing the dual demands of family and career—with flextime, sequencing, job sharing, working at home, and other alternatives to traditional career paths. The debate on the "mommy track" rages on, and although there's some confusion about *how* to bring about change, it's heartening that corporations are taking seriously the goal of promoting women in the corporate hierarchy. More and more companies are looking seriously at any and all ways to hold on to and advance their best employees—women.

The younger generation of men has been socialized to participate in running a home and rearing a family. This trend is due in part to people marrying later than they did a generation ago. The median age for first marriage is up, and many men live by themselves before marriage. Men are therefore more accustomed to cooking, cleaning and taking care of themselves today, whereas years ago men who went from mother to wife never needed to learn even how to boil water. A generation ago, professional women would abandon their careers if their husband had to relocate. Today it may be the husband who relocates if his wife gets an offer too good to pass up in a distant city.

Opportunities for women are beginning to open up in all areas. Women are entering business as well as government in unprecedented numbers. The 1984 Democratic party nominee for vice president, Geraldine Ferraro, was the first woman to be nominated to national office by a major party. Sandra Day O'Connor is the first woman to sit on the Supreme Court. Jeane Kirkpatrick was the first woman to be U.S. ambassador to the United Nations. Sally Ride and the late Judith Resnick were the first women astronauts in the United States.

In 1989, President George Bush picked Elizabeth Dole to be the head of the Labor Department. She was the second woman named to a cabinet or top-level position in the Bush administration, along with Washington, D.C., lawyer Carla Hills, who was named U.S. trade representative. Hills, as trade chief, will spend a good deal of time negotiating with the Japanese and other major trading partners. Maybe George Bush read this book and found out why women make the best negotiators in foreign markets! A third woman, former minority leader of the Wisconsin Senate Susan Engeleiter, now heads up the Small Business Administration.

In fact, women seem to have moved up faster in politics than in large corporations. Women appointees to state cabinet-level jobs are up 114 percent from 1981, whereas women hold only 5 percent of all executive positions. In the major corporations the percentage is even lower: Out of 50,000 top executives, only 1,000 are women. This is bound to change over time, however. The male executives now rising up the corporate ladder are much more comfortable with executive women than today's CEOs, in part because some of them are married to career women.

Today only a relative handful of women are presidents, CEOs, and chairs of large corporations. But these numbers are growing. In Washington, D.C., the American Stock Exchange, Avon Products, Coca-Cola, Control Data, Esmark, Gulf Oil, Hallmark Cards, Hershey Foods, and St. Joe Minerals all have lobbying offices headed by women executives. A recent dinner held at the American Stock Exchange in New York honored 150 prominent executive women who are top executives or owners of businesses earning over five million dollars a year.

One indicator of acceptance of women executives is shown by the increase in their number on corporate boards. Over 400 women now sit in the boardrooms of the most powerful corporations in the United States. Currently, Spencer Stuart and Associates, a New York recruiter, is conducting 23 searches for 11 corporate boards, 7 of which are specifically looking for women. Another indicator of change is the recent opening of prestigious, formerly all-men, private clubs to businesswomen.

While the number of women in business and the professions is growing rapidly in the United States, most countries overseas are just starting on the road to equality. Although women constitute 40 percent of Great Britain's labor force, they fill only 10 percent of its managerial posts. In 1984, however, the parliament in Switzerland—a country where women were given the right to vote only 13 years ago—chose a woman, Elisabeth Kopp, to be a cabinet minister for the first time in 136 years. She served until her resignation in 1988. Surprisingly, women hold 13 percent of managerial posts in Portugal, one of the poorer countries in Western Europe. Not surprisingly, women only hold 6 percent of managerial posts in Spain, a country that is still overwhelmingly macho.

A Ph.D. and European sales manager of a U.S. company sought venture capital funds to open her own computer company in London. She was repeatedly turned down by merchant bankers who felt that as a woman she would be unable to attract competent male professionals to work with her. She persevered and raised a then–British record of 2.1 million dollars for her start-up. Olivetti, the giant Italian office equipment company put up 25 percent. One progressive bank in Britain, National Westminister, is experimenting with a five-year program allowing women in management to take a leave for child raising. They wisely reasoned that without this type of program, they would lose out on talented women who chose not to stay or didn't join the company in the first place.

In 1989, media baron Rupert Murdoch sent American troubleshooter Patricia Mastandrea to London to help launch his Sky Television Satellite venture. Ms. Mastandrea, a chief operating officer of the company, is described as being "tough, very tough," an attribute she'll need in Britain to operate in "a clubby, male dominated world where female American executives are rare."

In 1984, Prime Minister Laurant Fabius of the Socialist government of France named Edwige Avice, 39, as the secretary of state of the Defense Ministry in his cabinet. In Germany, Petra Kelly, 36, is Nuremberg's Green Party representative to the German parliament.

In Italy, Maria Bellisario was the head of Italtel, the top telecommunications company, until her death in 1988. In Taiwan, Vivian Yen runs the Yue Loong Motor Company, one of the country's leading businesses.

While more opportunities for women in business and government are opening up in Western Europe, countries in the Far East are also beginning to see women advancing in the business world. As a result of rapidly growing industries such as electronics and textiles, women from rural areas in South Korea, Malaysia, Indonesia, the Philippines, Singapore, and Taiwan are flocking to the cities to work in factories. While this is only the beginning of a long process toward female careers, the increased literacy and later marriages that are resulting are providing the opportunity for young women to advance in the work force.

Japan, with a highly educated female population, prepares women for professional careers that in the past haven't gone very far up the corporate ladder. Only 1 of the top 16 executives in the Japanese Federation of Electrical Machine workers is a woman, even though one fifth of the 530,000 members are female. In the technical and professional areas, a shortage of male software engineers has sent company recruiters increasingly to the women's college campuses to seek personnel. Computer maker Fujitsu hired over 150 women software engineers in 1982. The result of the high-technology industrial revolution is one of the biggest fundamental changes to affect female career progress in Japan.

IBM Japan actively recruits young women. Although only 14 percent of the company's employees are women, and only 2 percent of management are women, this is still far more than in most Japanese high-tech companies. Japan's more than 16 million working women make up more than 35 percent of the labor force. In 1988, for the first time 75 percent of major Japanese corporations polled said they would be as likely to hire a woman as a man for the same position—impressive, considering that fewer than 33 percent gave that answer just before the country's first equal opportunity law went into effect in 1986. Keep in mind, though, that the law has no provision for penalties.

Notwithstanding this mixed record, I predict that there will be a shake-up in the next 10 to 15 years. Japan is in a situation similar to that of the United States 20 years ago: There is a highly educated and motivated female work force just waiting to get out of the kitchen. While Japanese culture may not allow for the radical aspects of a feminist movement, you will see an evolutionary process that will markedly increase the role of women in the Japanese work force over the next few years. The younger generation of women wants a career *and* a family—and they'll have it. Sound familiar? Wait and see.

In the Middle East, progress for women, while slower than elsewhere, is still real. The majority of women have not even made the limited progress of those in Western Europe or the Far East; but the chief of the Saudi Press Agency in Washington, D.C., is a U.S.-educated Saudi Arabian woman. While few Middle Eastern women hold positions outside the home, this is slowly changing. Banks and other businesses owned by women for women are becoming increasingly popular in the Arab world.

In a number of the Latin American countries, particularly Argentina, Brazil, Uruguay, and Chile, women are participating in the political and business world. In Brazil, Luiza Erundina de Souza was elected mayor of São Paulo in 1988. In Colombia, the minister for communications, Noemi Sanin Posada, is a young, well-educated, fairly high-level governmental official.

In almost all the capitals of Latin America, young women office workers are a common sight. They work side by side with men up to the level of lower management. There are still few women in middle and upper management, except of course in family-owned businesses. However, women as small-business owners are becoming common. Recent improvements in literacy, the influence of feminism from the United States and Europe, and a loosening of the traditional power of the church are beginning to make positive changes in the professional status of women in Latin America.

These gains and changes coming from all parts of the world are providing opportunities for U.S. women as never before. You will no longer be the first woman working in a particular company office in a capacity other than secretary. Governments, corporations, small companies, and schools are beginning to realize that women can do the job. It may still take twice the effort to get half the reward, but there is no question that the effort will lessen and the reward will increase. The more women in business and politics worldwide, the easier it will become to penetrate areas where women were previously excluded. But why the international arena?

"I am having a hard enough time getting ahead in a domestic company; why should I take on the added fight of dealing with foreigners who are even more resistant to women?" you may ask. The answer is that international business is the field of the twenty-first century. There will be more opportunities for women in global business because the international sector is growing, the rules are changing, and the pace is faster.

A 1989 article in the *Wall Street Journal* compared the qualifications for the chief executive officer of the year 2000 to his predecessor.

He would have an undergraduate degree in French literature but also a joint MBA/engineering degree. Experienced in marketing and finance [he] proved himself in a turnaround situation in Brazil. But unlike his predecessor he isn't a drill sergeant. He is first among equals in a 5 person office of the Chief Executive. The parochial predecessor with an accounting degree worked his way up through the company from the controller's office to running the division to the top dog. His management style was learned in the army. However, until he made CEO he had never traveled out of the country. He's afraid of computers and probably wears a polyester/wool blend suit!

One chief executive interviewed for the article said, "I'm glad I lived when I did.... the requirements for chief executives have changed." Single-function, single-country executives won't be the ones at the top. A follow-up article on future managers (those reporting to the CEO) explains that he *or* she will be computer literate, have a BA in literature, have a joint MBA/advanced communications degree, have worked abroad, and oversee offices on 4 continents.

The great industrial might of the United States went unchallenged for many years. The internal market could absorb all the output of our industries, and our natural resources were seemingly so abundant that we didn't need to import raw materials. But while U.S. industry ignored foreign markets, other countries, especially Japan and West Germany, began to see that the road to higher profits and production ran across national boundaries.

Japan's small size and Germany's proximity to other European nations forced these countries to be exporters. Japanese and German executives are old hands at dealing with foreign trade partners. The United States, on the other hand, is incredibly naive when it comes to international matters. Leonard A. Lauder, president and CEO of the cosmetics company Estee Lauder, once said that if we could get Americans to understand that not everyone in the world speaks English, we'd eliminate half the U.S. trade deficit.

In 1984, that trade deficit broke all records at 120 billion dollars. In 1988, the deficit dropped back to 120 billion dollars after having reached a record high of 152 billion dollars in 1987. Some of this had to do with the incredible strength of the dollar, which makes it easier for us to buy foreign goods than for people overseas to buy U.S.-made products. Another factor is the debt situation of the developing world. U.S. executives also complain about various forms of protectionism which they claim unfairly keep our goods out of many foreign markets. But a significant part of the problem has to do with the simple fact that most U.S. executives simply don't know how to do business with foreign executives.

As one executive was recently quoted, the United States is the only country "that makes a distinction between business and international business." This lack of understanding, combined with a serious dose of ethnocentrism, has cost U.S. companies millions of dollars. We still try to sell our left-hand-drive cars to countries where people drive on the left side of the road and need right-hand steering. Up untill recently, advertisements for refrigerators in the Middle East could be found depicting the shelves full of ham, while the refrigerator companies wondered why Moslems (who are forbidden to eat pork) bought refrigerators from West Germany or Japan instead.

The stories of marketing blunders are legend. General Motors test-marketed the Chevrolet Nova in Latin American markets, not considering the fact that "no va" means "It doesn't go" in Spanish. The campaign bombed spectacularly. Less well-known blunders include the large multinational corporation that attempted to sell baby food in an African nation by using the same labels as in the U.S. market, which showed a picture of a baby. African consumers took a look at the product and were horrified: They thought from the labels that the jars contained ground-up babies. Pillsbury's Jolly Green Giant was originally translated as the "intimidating green ogre" in Saudi Arabia. Later, a more liberal translation produced the "Giant of the Valley," which no doubt sold more vegetables.

Many foreign companies have taken over markets that once were ours, not only because their products are superior or even less expensive, but because they know how to sell to consumers who don't share their language and culture. U.S. companies tried in the past to sell products overseas that had been designed for the U.S. market, instead of researching what kind of products overseas consumers wanted. We made top-loading washing machines, so we tried to export top-loading washing machines. No one seemed to pay attention to the fact that women in Latin America, who tend to be shorter than women in the United States, are more comfortable with front-loading washing machines. When any effort at all was made to accommodate our products to overseas markets, it was by *retrofitting*—taking a finished product and tinkering with it to make it acceptable to overseas consumers. No one ever thought of designing a new product with a foreign market in mind.

Even when U.S. products were suitable for export, and weren't advertised in a way that turned off their intended consumer, many sales were lost because the managers responsible for selling them didn't speak the language of the buyers or didn't understand international negotiating. In many cases, the only thing U.S. companies exported was their markets, which were taken over by foreign producers who made products designed with their customers' cultures in mind, and who understood how to "massage" their negotiating partners.

All this has begun to change, largely because U.S. executives' lack of intercultural understanding has hurt their companies right on the bottom line. Change is coming slowly, and old beliefs persist. Twenty years ago, when worldwide competition wasn't so fierce, U.S. goods were unanimously regarded as the best in the world. Nobody then would have thought of buying Japanese goods for their quality. All that is reversed now, and U.S. companies are trying hard to catch up. Business schools are just beginning to realize the importance of international negotiating, and a few of the more sophisticated and progressive schools have initiated courses on the subject.

Today the extent of global competition is such that U.S. companies are beginning to become much more flexible and global in their strategic planning. Many U.S. companies are shifting their manufacturing activity abroad. Some big companies are giving up production of key products to foreign companies altogether, and are acting as marketing agents instead. Some companies are attempting to cut costs by buying cheaper foreign-made components whenever possible. The United States has become the leading importer of foreign goods. U.S. imports were projected to value at nearly $475 billion dollars in 1989.

Exporting, while important, is difficult and seems for many large companies to be less cost-effective than investing in manufacturing overseas, except in industries where a new technology is in demand and price is not an issue. Even in these cases the competition is strong from other industrialized nations. Price is less of an issue when long-term relationships between seller and buyer exist. In many countries throughout the world, no business is conducted, no matter what the price, unless a personal relationship exists. Developing these relationships is time-consuming and costly, but the expense is preferable to doing no business at all.

It's ironic that in an era of depersonalizing electronic communications, the face-to-face meeting and the handshake to seal the transaction are more important than ever. In the years to come, opportunities for trade will come from all corners of the world. U.S. executives, if they are savvy in international negotiating, will see a big demand for their products and services in the Far East, Western Europe, and Latin America. We are beginning to see more combinations of global joint ventures, deals, mergers, trades, and countertrades than ever before. This is likely to continue for a long time, providing unlimited opportunities in the international marketplace. Women who know their industry and learn to negotiate are the best candidates to succeed in these overseas ventures.

2

Preparing for Your Career in International Business

How do you prepare yourself properly for a career in international business? There are two basic paths that you can choose. One is to select an area of business, such as marketing, finance, management, or whatever interests you; study for it; practice it domestically; and when you are quite competent in your field, learn about how to apply it in the international arena. The other path is to begin thinking internationally as you start to prepare for your career.

In a world that is shrinking rapidly even as it is growing more competitive, you're better off thinking internationally at the outset. But if you have already prepared yourself for a career in domestic business, you can become knowledgeable about the international side of your specialty within a relatively short time. Many U.S. companies already have multinational, international, or global operations in which you can apply the skills you have already practiced in the domestic division and, as I will discuss in Chapter 10, many U.S.-based firms are being acquired by foreign owners, giving you an opportunity to work in the United States with overseas managers. The United States is also host to hundreds of foreign companies that need skilled managers to run their U.S. subsidiaries. All these trends will continue for the long term.

Training for a career in international business could begin as early as grade school with the study of foreign languages. Not all of us are lucky enough to get such an early start. But certainly by the time a young person who aspires to a career in international business is in college, a portion of the curriculum should be devoted to one or more foreign languages and to other international studies.

As the world is shrinking, so is the need for generalists in management. You simply cannot specialize in international business alone; you must acquire hard skills in a growing area, such as marketing, sales, accounting, finance, computer science, or engineering. You can then apply these skills to the international field.

International courses should be taken as a minor, or even better, as a dual major on the undergraduate or graduate business school level. These course areas might include international trade and finance, international marketing, international economics, legal and tax aspects of international business, and so on. These courses, which are taught in most business schools, are all very important. However, perhaps the most important subject, international business negotiating, is taught in only a handful of schools, such as the University of Pennsylvania and New York University (NYU). While not specifically international in scope, any courses on sales and entrepreneurship are also valuable as they focus on the personal and motivational aspects of business. These skills are vital in an international business career.

If you have already finished your education it may not be necessary to go back to school to get another college degree. However, if you are not already experienced in the international marketplace, I recommend that you take at least a few courses or seminars, or even a certificate program, in some aspect of international business. Many universities offer excellent programs in their continuing education or extension divisions. For example, since 1985 I have chaired a seminar at New York University's School of Continuing Education called "Conducting Business in the World Marketplace: New Opportunities for Women." The course has attracted women representing every area of domestic business.

If you are still in school, international expertise is not hard to acquire today, as almost all business schools now have international tracks. Many law schools offer programs including multinational business transactions and taxation, and courses in comparative law (studying the legal systems of other countries). Many schools of government and public administration also offer international programs.

Half of the 1984 class at NYU's Graduate School of Business Administration are women; 20 percent of these women are studying in an international business concentration along with their finance, marketing, computer, or accounting tracks. In a survey, 52 percent of women indicated that they would be willing to relocate for advancement, and 43 percent said they would be willing to travel frequently for business. Their attitudes indicate a growing trend toward interest in international business.

Additionally, there are schools that specialize in the international (management) field such as the American Graduate School of International Management (better known as Thunderbird) in Arizona. Over 300 schools in every part of the United States have some form of international program.

While some of these schools offer only a few international courses, the majority of schools offer undergraduate business degrees with a concentration or major in international finance, management, marketing, or economics. Many of these schools also offer master's degree programs, and some have doctoral programs in international business. While these programs are by no means uniform or standardized, there are enough schools in every region for you to choose a recognized program.

The very popular Master's of Business Administration (MBA) may or may not be for you. But by all means look at the alternatives to it before committing to two to four years of study. Some universities offer certificate programs in their continuing education or extension divisions. New York University has one such program that can train you in a number of business functions without the investment of many years of study.

You may be interested in other skill/function areas that are ancillary to business, such as law, media, travel and tourism, computer technologies, anthropology, science, or engineering. There is tremendous opportunity for these skills overseas. Business courses should be taken together with these majors to provide the necessary proficiency. On the other hand, degrees in business, whether graduate or undergraduate, should always be taken with liberal arts courses. Nobody really wants to do business with a bean counter, so learn about the arts and humanities to add depth and sophistication to your business acumen.

A number of schools also offer internships overseas or study abroad programs. If time and money are not barriers, you should by all means enroll in these programs to get some direct experience with a foreign language and culture. One way to get experience is to be an unpaid intern in an international division of a U.S. corporation, a foreign firm, or an import-export company. In this way, you can learn all you can in a short period of time and parlay that knowledge into a salaried position. The pay may be low or nonexistent, but the exposure could be just the thing to get you hired after graduation.

When you graduate, you may be fortunate enough to find a job in a corporation that will train you for international business. But don't look only for international jobs at the beginning of your career, even if you have concentrated on international courses in business school. You can always practice your specialty domestically for a while and then go international.

The job of transition to, or entry into, international business is easier if you already have the requisite soft (or cultural) skills. If you are already a manager or executive in a domestic operation, take some courses in international businesss and then learn about a particular area of the world and its culture. You are then ready to apply for a transfer or a new job in an international division. If you are a woman who is just beginning a business career, consider management traineeships. Such positions in large international companies and banks are another way to obtain valuable experience. For women who are entering a second career in business after a traditional career such as social work, teaching, or nursing, an internship or traineeship program may make the transition to international business easier than you'd think.

Some areas that are often overlooked are training and human resources (formerly called personnel). These used to be "female ghettos" in most large firms, but they have become two of the hottest growth areas for the 1990s. A new specialization called manager of diversity and based in the human resources areas calls on skills at which women are best. This position deals with sensitizing the work force to the gender, race, and culture differences that are part of the modern office.

Nowadays women are frequently groomed to take over the family business, a province once exclusively reserved for men. If you are in the enviable position of having a family business, you might want to examine the possibility of expansion or exporting to overseas markets. Since we know that women's negotiating ability is best matched to foreign cultures, a business previously headed up by an older male may now be at just the point for overseas growth.

Combine your communication or people skills with some hard international and management skills and some cultural and language training, and take an entry-level job to start. One former high-school language teacher took a low-paying job in an international sales organization, and then worked her way up to one of the top sales jobs in the company.

There are other ways to get into business if you don't have a long track record. A middle manager at a bank owes her career to a stint as an executive "temp." While temporary positions have traditionally involved low-level functions, there is a whole new industry in "temping" at the managerial level. When she couldn't find suitable work after completing a career-change MBA, the manager took a temporary position in the international division of a top bank. The management was so pleased with her skill that they offered her a full-time job—and a promotion.

Many women are still reluctant to be aggressive when it comes to their careers, and feel instead that they will eventually be recognized for their ability. This attitude, like other old myths, is falling by the wayside, however. In international as well as domestic business the way to succeed is to learn a skill, develop a confident personality (even if you have to fake confidence at first), and gain total expertise in the products or service you are selling. But once you have achieved this foundation, you must be assertive and push for the assignments you want and for the promotions you deserve. Quietly waiting for recognition will no longer succeed (if it ever did). Become visible in your field. Write articles and give speeches. It's the best way to promote yourself.

Another avenue of self-promotion is networking. Join an organization in your field or even a charitable group. Speak to everyone you meet there and get yourself on a committee. Seeing your name in print (even if it's in the organization newsletter) can be helpful. Your name in print provides the halo effect. Use any article you've written or any mention of your name to get your name in print elsewhere. Try it, it works!

Another boost to your career is to find a mentor. For quite a while it was difficult for a woman to find a woman mentor because most of the senior positions were occupied by men, but today you can be mentored by someone of either sex. Often the best way to go about this is to ask someone for an introduction to the executive you would like to be your mentor. Mentoring can be done in a variety of methods; there is no one formula. It may take the form of an informal meeting with someone who gives you advice on the industry or function in which you're interested. It may take the form of an in-house relationship in which your mentor trains, sponsors, or generally takes you under his or her wing; or it can be anything in between. Look into any alumni-sponsored mentoring programs. For many years I have been an alumni mentor at the Pace University (N.Y.) Graduate School of Business. I specifically request women protégées because women need a role model who is successful in the still male-dominated international arena. You should ask to be mentored, as few people will come to you unasked.

If you are considering changing careers or returning to the workplace, the international field may be the arena for you. Age is not a handicap here. In fact, in many countries throughout the world, older really is better. Certain cultures venerate age and may be more willing to listen to an older person.

While women are not yet totally accepted in all areas of business, whether domestic or international, there is widespread agreement that women are often better than men at negotiation. Women are generally more verbal and flexible. They tend to view the negotiating process as part of a long-term relationship. Because these skills of patient negotiating are so vital in an international setting, a 45- to 50-year-old woman with hard professional skills may often be the best candidate to negotiate a high-powered international deal.

The only other attribute such a woman would need to succeed in the international arena is a strong background in soft or cultural skills. In our culture, women more than men have been socialized from early childhood to be dependent on others. Therefore, it is often easier for a women to understand and internalize the importance of culture in the international marketplace. In contrast, there are men who still believe that the soft skills are not necessary when doing business overseas, much to the detriment of their companies' bottom line.

Cross-cultural skills can be learned both by face-to-face experience and through research or schooling. If you vacation in other countries, try to learn something of the culture and lifestyle of the local population. Observe people at their daily tasks. This may not be sufficient for a career in international business, but it's certainly a start. If you have an interest in a particular region, focus on it. I say region, because it is best to specialize in a region rather than a single country in order to maximize your professional opportunities. Be sure to learn the differences between countries in that region. Argentina is as different from Brazil as Italy is from France.

A good idea is to specialize in the Pacific Rim countries or the European Community. These are very popular growth areas for the 1990s. If you are interested in Asia, learn Japanese or Chinese—or some of both. Learn the cultural differences between the major countries and find out what areas of business are booming. With the consolidation of the European Community in 1992, there will be enormous opportunities for expansion of all types of business within Europe (see Chapter 6). Learn or practice French, Italian, and Spanish, and know Britishisms as well.

Learning a foreign language is one of the most important cultural skills you can acquire. The Japanese and many Western Europeans are amazed at how few Americans know other languages. Few U.S. colleges still require foreign language study, which is simply not perceived as what it really is—a requirement for global competitiveness in business. The U.S. position in foreign trade needs all the edge it can get. Our narrow-minded attitude toward foreign language can best be summed up by a congressman who opposed a bill to provide 150 million dollars in grants for teaching foreign languages, and declared, "If Jesus Christ spoke English, it's good enough for me."

Americans must learn foreign languages unless we want to continue abandoning our export markets to the Japanese, Germans, and other foreigners. Many international executives from all parts of the world speak fluent English and have at least a passing knowledge of the culture of the United States. Approximately 95 percent of the Japanese who do business in the United States speak English. In contrast, only perhaps 1 percent of Americans doing business in Japan speak Japanese. You don't need to be fluent; a bit of conversation will open many doors.

Many Americans have language-learning fears similar to the well-known math fear. While it is ideal to learn a foreign language before puberty, there is no reason that you can't learn a foreign language with some skill at any time in your life. There are literally hundreds of language programs offered in most large cities, from inexpensive group classes to individual total-immersion courses. Records, tapes, and books are an inexpensive way to begin learning or to refresh your knowledge of a language. In many large cities, there are also foreign language programs on radio and TV.

There are any number of ways to learn the language and the culture of a country or region. In many cities there are associations such as the Brazilian American Society, Japan House, Goethe Haus (German), and the Alliance Française, which offer the opportunity to learn a language and converse with native speakers. These organizations sponsor not only language classes, but also cultural seminars, social events, cooking classes, and trips to restaurants, museums, and movies, all of which can help you to learn the language of a foreign country and also its cuisine, social customs, literature, and history.

In addition, most large cities have foreign-owned restaurants, foreign-language movie theaters, and stores that carry magazines and newspapers in foreign languages. If you live in any large city you can eat a different ethnic cuisine every night for at least a month! Learning a foreign language and culture are not necessarily easy, but they can certainly be enjoyable.

Some of the languages and cultures most in demand in international business today are Japanese, Russian, and Chinese. These languages are particularly difficult to learn for Americans, as are their cultures. French, Spanish, and German are also still extremely important languages to learn for international business, and they are somewhat easier to learn because they are written in the familiar Roman alphabet and because many words in these languages are closely related to English words. Also, the cultures of European countries are more familiar to most of us than the cultures of Asia or the Middle East. While you do not necessarily need to speak a language fluently in order to have a successful career, you will increase your chances overseas if you speak another language at least passably.

There is no way to learn everything about another culture except by living in it for a good deal of time. But you must learn the most important points. Literally millions of dollars in business have been lost by American businessmen who didn't observe the most fundamental rules of another culture and alienated their foreign hosts. Such acts as using the left (bathroom) hand or showing the sole of the shoe in Arabic society, looking a Japanese contact deeply in the eyes, touching an Asian, or recoiling in horror at being hugged or kissed by a Latin or Arab are the best-known examples of offensive ignorance. Many far more subtle mistakes made by Americans have cost dearly. Impatience in negotiating—what we see as wanting to "put the cards on the table"—is seen in almost all other cultures as rude and boorish.

Perhaps the single most important idea in conducting international business is the variable concept of time. Many cultures throughout the world view time different from Americans. In the United States, a meeting set for 10:00 A.M. will begin no later than 10:15. In some parts of the world, it may begin hours later. In Mexico, local executives will often jokingly specify whether the time set for a meeting is *hora Mexicana* or *hora Americana*.

To do business in other countries, you must get to know your contact or host. Without this personal familiarity, negotiations will never be taken seriously. We in the United States do a great deal of business on the telephone, through the mail, and in other impersonal ways. Overseas, nothing will ever replace the face-to-face meeting. It is not uncommon for us to call someone by his or her first name over the phone or at a first meeting. This will not work in most foreign countries. To conduct serious business overseas, a long-term relationship of trust must be established.

Most Americans find it very difficult to attend meetings where little or no business is discussed. They see this process as a waste of time and therefore boring, or think they are being put off. Nothing could be further from the truth! Your hosts are trying to get an understanding of who you are as a person before they will commit themselves to negotiating the terms of the business deal.

Be prepared, and prepare those to whom you report, to spend a good deal of time without immediate gratification (i.e., sales). Relationships must be cultivated over a period of time. This is easier for women than for many men. Another vital concept in dealing with many other countries is that of family relationships. The extended family (almost unknown in the United States today) is the focus of social life in many areas, particularly in Latin America and Arabic cultures. The welfare of these family members may take priority over the scheduled meeting with you. Broken or postponed appointments can occur in these cultures, and again, women (even in sexist Arabic countries) have somewhat of an edge in dealing with these problems. Concern for family members has, up until recently, been the responsibility of women in American society. Your tolerance of these and other ambiguous norms will result in your gaining acceptance and trust. The time spent allowing your client to get to know you will be well worth it when you come back to your home office, contract in hand!

3

Careers in International Business

In today's business world, the road to the executive suite often passes through the international division. As far back as 1979, in a poll of *Fortune* 500 executives (both male and female), almost 70 percent said that international experience is a requirement for promotion to top management. These executives agreed that international experience is especially important in a company whose CEO is in charge of both domestic and international operations. More than half said that international experience would be important even in selecting the head of a purely domestic division. More recent surveys show that international experience is still regarded as an important qualification for senior management.

Ten years ago, very few women were in international positions either stationed overseas or traveling from a home-office base. Today, while the percentage of expatriate women managers is still fairly low, the number of women traveling overseas on business is booming.

Since women are entering every type of career domestically, areas of international business that were previously male-dominated are also opening up. This pressure on corporations results from equal opportunity legislation, from women's high levels of education, and (most of all) from the tremendous drive on the part of women, which has produced gains in domestic responsibility as well as in the international sector. Many major corporations are rethinking their policies, and have realized that unless women can advance and grow in their careers, both the women and the corporations stand to lose. The enormous pool of high-quality talent represented by women in the work force has had a positive effect on the economic situation in the United States, especially at the higher end. In families with incomes between $40,000 and $50,000, more than 70 percent of the women now hold jobs.

Women are now requesting overseas posts and positions requiring frequent travel because we know that is the way to the executive suite. A recent survey of top managers in the United States and overseas asked what qualities the CEO of the year 2000 will need; one of the chief qualities listed was "a vision about the company's strategic position in a global environment."

"If I were offered any job I wanted in a company and I didn't know that company well," wrote Mark McCormick, author of *What They Don't Teach You at Harvard Business School*, "I would ask to head the international division. All else being equal, this is probably where I could make the most impact in the least amount of time."

The place where women must do the most convincing is not overseas, where initial resistance can be broken down, but in the home office. For some women stationed overseas, managing in a foreign country may be less of a problem than the resistance from the home office, where top management is very sensitive to what foreigners think of women. Until recently, most male executives simply assumed that foreign businessmen were accustomed to more male-dominated cultures and would be resistant to doing business with women from the United States. However, most foreign businessmen are actually no more reluctant to do business with an American woman than with an American man. In 1981, Xerox Corporation's Chinese operation was headed by a woman. SUNOCO Overseas (a subsidiary of the Sun Oil Co.) and Southeast First National Bank of Miami both have had women heading their operations in Latin America in recent years. Women have also headed up General Electric in Moscow and Bank of America in Tokyo and Beijing. Suzy Ho heads Chase Manhattan Bank's private banking group in Tokyo. These are just a few examples of postings that would have been unthinkable 15 years ago but are increasingly common today. Women can function well in business, even in the most macho cultures.

This is not to say that the picture for women is altogether wonderful. (Is it ever?) Women are still underrepresented in international business on all levels, but they are making superb gains. Unfortunately, with all the lip service given to professional quality in the United States, there are still a lot of unliberated males in upper levels of management. These are the people who must be convinced that qualified women can not only match the performance of males overseas, but can far exceed them in almost all international business ventures.

In a 1984 Gallup poll of almost 500 female executives, only 35 percent reported spending as many as 5 days a month traveling for business. Even women in domestic positions reported the same problem: Management's fear that even U.S. businessmen won't deal with U.S. businesswomen on an equal footing.

Of course, many of these fears about how someone else will react to women managers are only expressions of a male boss's own sexist attitudes. Projecting these antifeminist attitudes onto unseen others is a means, whether conscious or subconscious, of making a male executive's sexist feelings seem more acceptable to himself or to his subordinates. (Of course, the courts have held in many cases under the equal employment opportunity laws that resistance by a company's customers to doing business with women is no excuse for the company to deny women equality in hiring, training, or promotions).

The way to overcome these attitudes is to confront the issue with the person or persons in charge, request travel responsibility, and prove that you can succeed. If your efforts are resisted, ask for reasons and attempt to enlighten management when all the old dinosaurs are presented. Support your argument with facts about women who have succeeded overseas, and ask for a chance to prove yourself. While you can't become "one of the boys"—nor would you want to—a good way to break down barriers is to get involved in sports. If you're interested, golf, tennis, squash, and other sports in which corporate men participate provide an excellent opportunity for you to network and keep fit.

There are certain industries that have traditionally promoted women and moved them into positions of prominence more easily than others. Women have gained overseas experience in publishing, banking, travel and tourism, and retailing, probably because there have been many women in the domestic branches of these industries for many years. Women in these fields have moved into positions of international responsibility faster than in other industries because of their already greater numbers and visibility in the home office.

But what about all the other industries? If you already work in a large multinational corporation, bank, insurance company, consulting firm, advertising agency, or accounting firm, and want to get into the international field, you may have the opportunity within your own company. Almost all large U.S. corporations have either an overseas subsidiary, an international division or branch, or at least some overseas clients or suppliers.

If you work in a smaller company that deals only with domestic clients, you will have to change to a company within your field that is international in scope. If you are not already settled in a career, be sure to look for jobs with international potential, but don't turn down a solely domestic job if it is in your area of expertise. You can always change employers after you've gotten some solid domestic experience. It's often said that a good sales rep can sell anything. It's equally true that a good sales rep can sell anywhere.

If you're not already established in a particular field, one of the best places to look for a career is within a service industry. The U.S. economy is rapidly becoming service-oriented. While manufacturing is declining, the service sector already accounts for three quarters of total U.S. employment. In the 1980s the service sector accounted for virtually all the growth in U.S. employment. Industries supplying business and consumer services, such as advertising, consulting, and hotels, have been reporting their best business in years. In large cities throughout the United States, service companies are becoming the largest employers. Over the next ten years, six out of seven new jobs will be in services; the Bureau of Labor Statistics estimates that service industries will generate 20 million new jobs by the year 2000.

This trend is also true internationally. The international market of invisible (i.e., service) trade is estimated at 700 billion dollars annually! U.S. service exports totalled over $90 billion in 1988.

The fields of banking, publishing, and retailing, which are front runners for women in international business, are all service-related industries. A few years ago I participated in a seminar at New York University, called "American Women: Distinguished International Careers," with seven other women, representing the fields of marketing, banking, retailing, executive recruiting, investments, government, consulting, and education. We represented a cross-section of international careers in service industries, and discussed the huge potential for women in these fields.

Perhaps the fastest track to the top corporate executive jobs is in sales and marketing. In a 1984 survey taken by Heidrick and Struggles, an international executive search firm, almost a third of the CEOs of nonindustrial (service) firms had backgrounds in marketing or sales.

While marketing and sales jobs are closely related, they often have very different career paths. Traditionally, there are a set number of steps up the corporate ladder within the consumer marketing arena. These may include assistant product manager, associate product manager, product manager, brand manager, marketing manager, director of marketing, marketing vice president, and so on. In smaller corporations, one or more of these steps may be omitted. In sales, on the other hand, there is no such direct hierarchy, but there may still be many steps to the top levels. It is occasionally difficult for a sales person to cross over into management, but many sales people stay out of management because of the flexibility and challenge they find in direct selling.

Related to marketing and sales are the fields of advertising and market research. These two areas have literally exploded in the international arena. With all the debate about global advertising and world brands, international advertising and market research have opened up significantly. Spending on international advertising is expected to increase more than 10 percent in 1989 alone. Women have traditionally been fairly visible in both advertising and marketing research, but for many years they were concentrated at the lower end. For example, advertising women were frequently clustered at the account executive level. Recently, women have begun to emerge in small but growing numbers as vice presidents and creative directors. Women have also been extremely successful as owners of their own advertising agencies. The demand for high-quality marketing research has created top-level positions in the market research companies as well as internal departments in corporations.

Among the newest trends in market research is observational research, which moves away from additional quantitative techniques and borrows qualitative methods from fields such as ethnography, cultural anthropology, psychology, and sociology. For women who have backgrounds in the social sciences, this is an excellent opportunity to cross over into a business career.

Publishing and media, industries in which women have long held many important domestic positions, are now beginning an international explosion. U.S.-based cable television networks have been signing lucrative deals in Europe and the Far East. Other U.S. media (films, records, syndicated television shows, etc.) are finding increasing audiences overseas, especially in Europe. The opportunities for women who have already begun to succeed in domestic media are enormous.

In smaller companies the pay may not be as high as in the large corporations, but a marketing/sales person may get more visibility early on. For those who don't care to to through the traditional steps of consumer and bank marketing, a job with a smaller company may be the way to move up quickly. You might take a marketing position in a small domestic or international company, gain visibility and experience for a few years, and then move on to a larger international-oriented company and circumvent years of small steps.

Sales experience is a transferable skill. If you are a strong closer, you can parlay that experience into the international sales market whether you're selling shoes or capital equipment. There is still some residual reluctance on the part of women to go into direct sales as a career because of the bad press given to salesmen in years past. Fortunately, sales persons have become a good deal more sophisticated and educated. Almost gone are the days of the pinky-ringed, white-belted, white-patent-leather-shoe salesmen. About 20 percent of all new hires in non-retail sales in 1988 were women. One of the most successful car salespersons in the United States is a woman. Sales executives, as they are now called with their higher levels of education, sell everything from sophisticated financial products to intangible services. Many college graduates feel they don't need an education for sales or that sales is not what they were trained for. Nevertheless, sales is an excellent place to learn quickly and efficiently how to negotiate business deals. While you must be internationally savvy to negotiate sales overseas, it doesn't take an advanced degree to learn a language and culture. Sales experience, cultural knowledge, and communication skills are all you need to succeed. If you feel you have the aptitude for sales, don't be reluctant to try this field. In a recent survey, 40 women at a seminar in international marketing said that contacts and interpersonal relationships are the most important factors for success in international marketing. Previous work experience, speaking a foreign language, formal education, and willingness to move were rated next most important.

The second most common backgrounds in the executive suite are finance and accounting, representing more than one fourth of the CEOs surveyed in the Heidrick and Struggles study. The most common entry-level position in finance is a financial analyst at a commercial or investment bank. Traditionally, analysts then move through the ranks of lower and middle management, much the way the consumer-goods marketer does. There is a lot of money to be made in investment banking, particularly if you manage the assets of wealthy individuals or corporations either here or abroad. While women have only recently begun to reach vice president and higher levels, there is definitely a trend toward more women in investment banking. With the influx of foreign capital to the United States as foreign investors seek high interest rates and a stable political climate, the international positions in investment banking are now more numerous than ever. Today, women hold more than 53 percent of all professional posts in the top banks.

Women have always had a fairly strong presence in commercial banking, and are beginning to emerge in high positions in international lending. Training in credit and skill at negotiating are the major requisites for high-level jobs as international lenders or commercial loan work-out specialists.

Accounting has seen a huge influx of women in the United States in the last 15 years. There are now close to 500,000 female accountants, or 39 percent of the nation's total, compared with only 160,000 in 1970. Although the most highly sought-after jobs are in the Big Five accounting firms, many smaller firms also have international clients. The most obvious choices for finance and accounting professionals are banks, brokerage firms, and accounting firms, but there is also a tremendous amount of opportunity in corporations of all sizes and in all industries for women with these skills.

The information explosion has opened up a vast array of jobs in computer and information sciences, which are commonly known as MIS (management information science). This area includes opportunities from entry-level data processing to executive-level managerial positions. Companies in all industries are automating their operations with amazing rapidity. All forms of communications jobs offer extremely fast-changing careers, and because MIS is a relatively new field, it shows great promise for advancement for women. Women have always held betwen 20 and 30 percent of professional computing jobs (as programmers and systems analysts), and, more important, women in the computer field earn dollar for dollar what their male colleagues earn, unlike in most other industries.

Today, 19 percent of engineering students and almost 40 percent of technical students are women. Female scientists and engineers accounted for over 50 percent of the increase in the number of college graduates in those fields between 1976 and 1983. Only 10 percent of high-tech managers are women, but this is sure to increase. Large high-tech corporations such as AT&T and Hewlett-Packard are promoting more female scientific managers and engineers; and women are heading a significant number of smaller companies in the biotech, medical, pharmaceutical, and electronics fields. There is still some difficulty in finding women who have both management and technical skills, but that is changing rapidly. While 12 percent of all CEOs currently come from the engineering field, the influx of computer, communications, and information companies will cause sharp increases in that number in the 1990s.

The 22 percent of CEOs who come out of manufacturing/operations probably never thought that women would encroach on their territory, but even on the traditionally male-dominated plant floor, women are beginning to rise into positions of influence. General Electric has a special program to train future manufacturing managers; 20 percent of the employees in the program are women.

The broad areas known as management and administration are somewhat difficult to pin down. According to the Census Bureau, the percentage of women employed as management analysts increased from 25 percent in 1970 to 45 percent in 1980. This statistic includes the traditional women's areas such as personnel, human resources, employee benefits and pensions, and general staff administration. For example, although only 25 percent of executive search professionals are now women, a recent study predicted that this number will double in five years. While somewhat downgraded in the past, these areas are beginning to take on new importance as the more glamorous organizational-behavior professionals with graduate and doctoral degrees enter these fields. The quality of work life and productivity have become major issues in corporations throughout the United States.

But perhaps the greatest opportunity may be in owning your own business and taking it into the international sector. More than 3.5 million women in the United States own their own businesses, which generate over $40 billion a year. Over 45 percent of these businesses are in services—the great strength of our economy. Women are often opening their own businessses because, like the immigrants to the United States earlier in this century, they are finding that this can be the fastest route into the mainstream. While a good percentage of these women-owned businesses are small, the drive and ambition of these women are huge, and so is the success that follows! Sales by women-owned businesses increased three times faster than those of male-owned businesses between 1977 and 1983. If current rates of business ownership by women continues, one study predicts, women could own half of all U.S. businesses by the year 2000.

Many women who open their own business are doing so by buying a franchise. One study showed that over 80,000 women in the United States are sole or part owners of franchises in fields ranging from diet and exercise to computers and fast food. There has also been a great increase in international franchising in the last few years. If you are involved in a franchise or franchisable business, you ought to seek out countries with consumer or business markets that would be suitable for your goods or services.

Don't overlook the many state, local, and federal government jobs that are international in scope. A short stint in an international government job can be a shortcut to rapid promotion when you return to the private sector. There are also some very satisfying long-term international careers in the government sector. For example, in the International Trade Administration of the Department of Commerce, there are jobs such as trade specialist in district offices, foreign commercial service officer, international economist, desk officer, and trade promotion specialist. Eximbank and OPIC (Overseas Private Investment Corporation) employ bankers and economists. The Agency for International Development (AID) and the State Department employ economists and investment development specialists. The United States Information Agency (USIA) hires officers to develop programs for visiting executives and diplomats. Other career opportunities exist in chambers of commerce, trade associations, export trading, and export management companies, as well as in multinational organizations including the United Nations and the International Monetary Fund, to name a few.

Law also offers many good opportunities for international careers. Over 8 percent of the CEOs of major corporations currently have legal backgrounds. A very good way for women to leapfrog the lower and middle levels of management is to become a lawyer, practice corporate law for a while, and then enter upper levels of management. There is still a somewhat intimidating quality to being a lawyer, and women lawyers are frequently good at negotiating. In international business this is a tremendous plus, and as a lawyer you will enter the corporate world with built-in status. If you choose to practice international law, there are many well-regarded international firms throughout the United States that deal almost exclusively with overseas clients or with the foreign legal problems of U.S. clients. Nearly all the larger U.S. law firms are now opening foreign offices, especially in Europe and the Far East.

No matter what field you choose, the only limit to your success is your drive and imagination.

4

Doing Business in the World Marketplace: An Introduction to International Negotiating

The United States of America is the greatest market in the world. With over 240 million people, three thousand miles between coasts, and a high standard of living, business opportunities are unlimited. Or so we in the United States thought until recently. Because of the great internal demand, there was little incentive to aggressively seek out business from other countries. Business came to us from all over the world.

Things have changed dramatically, and while the United States is still the leader in many industrial and nonindustrial sectors, quality competition is coming fast from all over the world. U.S. business is slowly beginning to realize that in order to continue being profitable, it has to focus more effort in overseas markets. The dollar has softened recently, and while imported goods have still been flooding the U.S. market, U.S. exports have become much more competitive pricewise.

Business is waking up to the fact that foreign competition is here to stay. U.S. industry used to think it could compete simply on a quality platform. We thought that because our goods were better than anyone else's, the countries of the world would come to us and we wouldn't have to market to them. Those days are over. In almost every industry, one or more foreign producers matches or surpasses our goods for quality or price. The Japanese make better and cheaper television sets, the West Germans make better cars, Brazil exports cheaper steel, and the Swiss make better chocolate. Because U.S. products can no longer compete successfully solely on quality or price, management is beginning to realize that the key to success in global marketing is in the selling.

To sell successfully you must first know your market. For a manager born and raised in the United States it is sometimes hard to recognize that consumers in Milan or Mecca have cultures vastly different from consumers in Minneapolis or Malibu.

The United States is a young country, and Americans pride themselves on having a democratic culture, with few class-based distinctions. Americans have no royal family and do not confer titles of nobility. We are not usually defined by our ancestry. While regional differences may be great, most Americans tend to minimize these differences and view themselves as being similar throughout the United States.

This accounts for the breezy, informal nature of doing business within this country. It is not uncommon for a businessperson to call a new contact three thousand miles away and begin using his or her first name during the first five minutes of the conversation. This practice is almost never regarded as insulting, but rather as an easy way to avoid wading through hours of getting acquainted. Even in complex negotiations, managers and executives in the United States often do not meet face-to-face until they are ready to close the deal.

Many foreign cultures are more formal and their societies are more stratified. In most other countries, there is a greater emphasis on polite, or even courtly, manners. Nothing gets done without many face-to-face meetings first. When business people meet overseas it is usually to open negotiations and to begin a long and complex relationship.

The failure to recognize these differences in culture, and the resulting differences in styles of doing business, cost U.S. industry millions of dollars each year in lost sales and lost opportunities.

In practically all countries throughout the world, but most importantly in the Middle East, Latin America, and the Far East, no business is conducted until and unless a foundation of trust has been established. This rule applies to any deal larger than selling a 79-cent replacement widget. Very little business is concluded through letters, calls, or telexes. These impersonal types of communications may be a good way to start a relationship, but only a series of sit-down meetings will result in the closing of any deal.

In overseas business one will almost never hear a conversation like this typical U.S. phone call:

"Interstellar Computer."
"Hello, may I speak to Barbara Smith?"
"This is Barbara."
"This is Pat Collins of American Biz Co. in New York. How's the weather in Los Angeles?"
"Oh, it's sunny and warm, what's it like in New York?"
"Cloudy and cold, Barbara, it's January. I understand that you are in the market for a software program for your telecommunications satellite. I have the perfect program for your operation."
"We usually get all our software from HiPrice Co., a company here in Malibu, Pat."
"Well, Barbara, I think we can beat their price and I'll send you our price list, a sample program, and specifications."
"Fine, Pat, I'd like to see them."
"O.K., call me when you get the information."
"Will do. Bye."
A week later:
"Hello, American Biz Co."
"Pat Collins, please."
"Pat Collins here."
"Hi, Pat, Barbara Smith here, how are you?"
"Just great."
"Pat, we read your price list and we'd like to order your Starpak."
"That's wonderful, I knew it was just right for Interstellar."
"I'll send you a check today."
"That's terrific, good talking to you."
"Bye-bye."

Doing business in this manner is common within the United States. This negotiating style is unique to this country, however. Although on the surface the dialogue sounds informal and spontaneous, the people involved are responding to a well-choreographed, culturally determined set of cues. While this style would never work overseas, a heavy-handed, more formal, and long-winded presentation would be a disaster in the United States, whether on the telephone or in person. This interchange works well because it is based on a series of accepted standards. Pat Collins doesn't really care about the weather three thousand miles away in Los Angeles, but the inquiry immediately establishes a feeling of camaraderie. Angelinos are personally proud of their unrelentingly sunny climate, while New Yorkers seem to take a preverse pleasure in continually griping about their weather. Briefly discussing the weather is a successful sales tool because it allows the buyer and seller to create a feeling of friendship.

This feeling is an illusion, of course. It is unlikely that the two women will ever even speak to each other again after this deal is over, much less meet face-to-face. But creating the appearance of friendship is important in our culture. (If both women were in the same city or region, the caller would begin with some other pleasantry.)

The caller next says that American Biz Co. knows that Interstellar is interested in software. It is obvious that she has done her homework. How did ABC know that Interstellar was buying software? Barbara Smith probably won't ask. Pat Collins smoothly assures her that ABC has the perfect program for her at a lower price than the competition. Price and quality are the selling points that count in our culture. Long-term relationships to establish trust are unnecessary for selling in the United States. Quality is fairly standard, and since competition is strong there is little reason to continue with a supplier if another one can provide a good product at the right price.

Nor is a personal relationship with a customer or a supplier necessary. Often it is not even possible; the United States is a very mobile society and people do not stay in the same place or job for long. Promotions within a company, change to other companies, and moves to other parts of the country are frequent. There are few patterns of family and friendship to produce relationships with inefficient suppliers.

In many regions of the world, personal relationships are the only basis for doing business. In some countries this practice has been carried to the extreme, and has produced widespread inefficiency and control of business by a few interlocking families. In other countries, while business is not controlled by a small group, few foreign suppliers will be able to penetrate the market without a long series of getting-to-know-you meetings. Although it is not always necessary to have a contact already in place, it certainly can speed up the negotiating process.

Negotiations in the United States, even those that involve large sums of money, have to do with agreeing on price and terms. In other parts of the world, negotiations are simply the beginning of a long process. A senior minister of Japan's Ministry of International Trade and Industry (MITI) advises, "To really get access to this [Japan's] market, you've got to learn the language and drink sake in nightclubs for 3 or 4 years. Can you find many American executives delighted to do this?" This long process may seem ridiculous to an American manager or executive who thinks only of the short-term bottom line. But the Japanese market is well worth the long-term investment, and U.S. businesses are beginning to learn how to get into it.

If you are beginning to cultivate contracts overseas, ask your business acquaintances in the United States if they know anyone in that country or region. Very often, just knowing a name in a particular country can help you. Better yet is a letter of introduction to a contact. This type of introduction is a highly effective way to cut down on long hours of establishing your credibility.

If you work for a large company, you can reduce introduction formalities in a number of ways. First, if your company is well known, its name alone is often enough to establish your credibility and to open some doors. Second, a large company often has branches, subsidiaries, or production facilities in place overseas. Third, given the globalism of large companies, they often have foreign nationals working in the U.S. headquarters office who can refer you to friends or business contacts in their country.

If you work for a small company and don't have any contacts already established overseas, begin corresponding with the person you will be meeting. At least three or four months before you meet, you should be writing regularly, telexing, faxing (if available), and calling if not prohibitively expensive. Letters should include brochures about your company and its products, polite inquiries about your contact's company, some brief information on your professional history, an expression of interest in your contact's "beautiful" country, and other low-key pleasantries.

All well and good, you may say, but what if I just found out that I'm going to Zagreb next week? Make quick inquiries to your business friends in the United States to find out if they know anyone at all in Yugoslavia. Next, immediately call or wire the person you're going to meet. Explain the reason for your hastily scheduled meeting and apologize for not having more time to prepare.

The reason that correspondence should begin in advance of your meeting is to begin developing a long-term relationship of trust. In most cases, deals aren't made nor are contracts signed at the first face-to-face meeting. If you have established in advance the fact that you are a woman (not all people in foreign countries will be able to know your sex from your name) you will make it easier at the first meeting. Your contact may have no problem doing business with you, but he may be surprised at seeing a woman if he thought he would be meeting with a man.

Do not expect to close a deal on the first meeting. It is the exception rather than the rule for this to occur. You may occasionally close a deal or get the contract on the first meeting in Germany or Switzerland, because in these countries executives rely more on written contracts and less on personal trust than elsewhere. But as a result, the terms of the deal and the language of the contract may be even more detailed than your original version.

On the other hand, you must be aware that in some parts of the world, the U.S.-style written contract does not mean the same thing as it does to us. In some countries it may not be an acceptable form of doing business at all. In the United States and in most European countries a contract is considered a binding obligation, but many cultures consider the idea of a written contract insulting. In others, a contract is considered a nonbinding expression of what both sides hope to achieve. In the Middle East, a person's word is even more binding than a written contract. To renege on one's word is unthinkable, and within Arab society deals are made and kept on a handshake. This is the reason for extensive face-to-face meetings. The client wants you to get to know him as much as he wants to get to know you. Mutual trust is the single most important basis for doing business in most parts of the Far East, the Middle East, and Latin America.

One of the major difficulties Americans have in negotiating overseas comes from the tendency to think we have a commitment when we don't. In Japan, it is considered insulting to say "no" flatly, so "yes" sometimes means "maybe" or even "probably not." Often when a "yes" answer is given, it is not in agreement to the terms offered, but only means that the proposal is understood. When a deal is finally closed between a U.S. and a Japanese company, the Japanese themselves often prefer that the contract be written in English to avoid this kind of ambiguity. They find that English is a better language for expressing the specific terms of a complex deal.

It is hard for some U.S. executives to understand how different the business culture of a foreign country can be. In the Middle East, all services, including the price of a taxi ride, are negotiated beforehand. In China, tips are often given before a service is performed to insure good service. These practices are very different from the accepted manner of doing business in the United States, where we do not negotiate beforehand or tip in advance. We assume that, for the most part, charges will be fair and within the market rate. In the United States, tips are given as a reward for good service, and withheld as a punishment for poor service.

While most Americans wouldn't think of going on a vacation without at least a sketchy knowledge of the country they're visiting, it rarely occurs to businesspeople to do research on these vital matters of doing business in a different culture.

One of the ways to smooth over less-than-cordial attitudes is to learn all you can about your client's business culture in whatever amount of time you have. If you are suddenly asked to leave for Colombia, China, or Czechoslovakia, run to the nearest library or bookstore and read whatever you find about the country—on the plane, if you have to. The more you know about a country, the better you'll be able to negotiate a deal. Of course, most assignments overseas are given in advance, so you will probably have an adequate amount of time to prepare yourself.

Learning about a country's history, politics, and social customs will show you how some current practices and attitudes have evolved. If you have the time, a good way to take an up-to-the-minute reading of the climate for women in general is to spend a day watching people go about their business. If you leave your home base on a Friday or Saturday and recover sufficiently from jet lag by Sunday, become a tourist for a day. Go to a park, museum, square, market, or store, and watch people interact. Even if women still walk behind the men, it doesn't mean it will be difficult for you, an American woman, to do business. But knowing current attitudes can help you to avoid making a major error. Try to know what major political and social trends are affecting the region in which you will be working. For instance, throughout the Middle East there has been a resurgence of Islamic fundamentalism that has had some effects even in liberal countries like Egypt. In parts of Europe, particularly Germany and some Scandinavian countries, there are some growing anti-American feelings concerning installations of nuclear weapons. In some parts of Latin America, there is resentment about the foreign debt and repayment situation. By understanding the current situations you provide yourself with knowledge that helps you to deal successfully.

The informality that characterizes U.S. business relationships is not shared or appreciated in most foreign cultures. While Americans are very serious about business, our domestic negotiating styles seem breezy and low-key to foreigners. When doing business in any other part of the world, do not call anyone by their first name unless you are invited to do so. Even in many Western European countries it is offensive to call someone by his or her first name. For example, people in Germany and France who have worked side by side for years may still call each other Mister or Miss.

In most countries, including Europe and the Middle East, you will be dealing with executives on the upper levels of management. There is less delegation of responsibility abroad than in the United States, and most high-level managers refuse to give up authority to middle managers. In the Far East there is somewhat more group decision making, but those involved are usually still on the upper levels of management. In negotiating, you cannot be too formal. Speak softly, clearly, and slowly. While many of your contacts will speak English well, they may not be able to understand rapid or colloquial English. More often than not, they will speak British English, which is the same for the most part but has important differences in vocabulary and usage.

For example, you can cause a lot of confusion in some countries if you try to put off discussion of a difficult issue by saying "Why don't we table that?" In the United Kingdom and in former British colonies, to table an issue doesn't mean to put it off for another time, but to put it on the table for discussion now. If you want to avoid confusion, use only standard English and say "With your permission, gentlemen, let's discuss this issue at our next meeting."

In most cultures, people do not get down to business very quickly. Preliminaries are decidedly formal until a genuine relationship of mutual respect and friendship has developed. In Latin America and the Middle East particularly, you must be prepared to sit down and drink coffee and discuss nonbusiness issues. But even a woman should not inquire about the wife and family of a Middle Eastern client; he would never discuss this at a business meeting. It is acceptable to say, "I hope your family is well," but leave it at that.

In Latin America you should discuss the cultural heroes, the beauty of the scenery, the rapid growth of the country and its industry, or sports. In the Middle East, the rapid growth of technology, the high quality of your lodgings and food, and the excellence of the coffee or tea are acceptable topics of discussion.

In Europe, while you may inquire after the family, it is not necessary to prolong small talk to the extent done in Latin America, the Far East, or the Middle East. Most Europeans speak English and other languages fairly well (and are continually amazed that most Americans do not speak any language beside English). You will probably be dealing with someone whose business card indicates their professional title (engineer, lawyer, Ph.D., etc.), as Europeans still consider management or administration less prestigious than the professions. In Italy, for example, most educated professionals are called *dottore* or *dottoressa* even if they don't have a Ph.D. or are not in medicine! Even if you're not sure if someone merits the title *dottore*, use it anyway. Your negotiating partners will be pleased at this flattery.

In the Far East and Southeast Asia, a good way to begin is to compliment people on the truly spectacular growth and development of the country. In Japan, a handshake is acceptable but a slight bow at the waist will be greatly appreciated.

In all countries, if you are offered coffee, tea, or a soft drink, accept it whether you want it or not. To refuse is an insult, particularly if the country prides itself on the excellence of their beverage.

Always allow your client to set the pace of the negotiations. Never try to hurry things along. Your knowledge of the host country, your intelligence and sensitivity, and the professionalism you bring to the meeting will be your greatest assets.

Women have a tremendous advantage over men in international negotiating. They very often are adept at reading nonverbal cues sent out during a negotiation. Studies show that men primarily pick up general ideas and conclusions from a conversation, while women often get more information from body language, intonation, voice pitch, and eye movements.

Moreover, the style of negotiating known as *pull*, in which you involve the other person in solving your mutual problem, is a skill many women have mastered. In a decision-making or negotiating situation, many women seek everyone's opinion and try to build consensus. When women do this at business meetings in the United States, male executives sometimes become impatient and frustrated at this seeming failure to "get to the point." But this is the negotiating style that succeeds in the Far East, Middle East, Latin America, and some European countries. Where American men are interested primarily in the outcome of the negotiation, women are interested in the process as well. A recent study at the University of Michigan showed that while males and females are equally adept at helping solve disputes, women tend to seek changes in future behavior while men push for immediate results. Women see themselves as "bridges"; men consider themselves "vises" forcing the sides together.

The pull style of negotiating allows for the expression of feelings in a non-adversarial way. Good negotiators build trust by allowing people to express their needs and feelings. The pull style of negotiating also includes paraphrasing what the other person has said, supporting the other person, and exploring the common ground.

Research has shown that the most successful negotiators are those chameleon-like men and women who seem most like their client or customer. The more closely matched the physical, social, and personality characteristics of the two negotiators, the more likely that a sale will occur. Women are of course physically different; however, the social and personal characteristics of U.S. women are often a far better fit with men of foreign cultures. Women, with their ability to involve and support, allow others to view themselves favorably. The more a negotiator can make prospective clients view themselves favorably, the more likely it is that they will reach agreement. Women are able to create a comfortable environment for their presentations because they have well-developed social skills. Women are more attentive and patient, compliment others more easily and naturally, and make friends more quickly than men.

All negotiations must take place in an atmosphere of trust and sincerity. The more trustworthy and believable the client perceives the negotiator to be, the more likely it is that a deal will be consummated. Women are frequently more open and candid than men. Very little business will take place overseas without trust, patience, and understanding. Women's avoidance of risk taking also finds them better prepared for the tasks of international negotiating. Successful women will take the time to learn about the client's needs, interests, preferences, and lifestyle without becoming impatient or seeming patronizing.

Another factor that helps women to succeed in international negotiating was noted by Michael F. Tucker, vice president of the International Division of Moran, Stahl, and Boyer in Colorado. As he observed: "American businesswomen usually have had to fight to get where they are. So they are often really outstanding people. They also tend to have better interpersonal skills, which are critical for adjustment to cross-cultural encounters."

A similar observation was made by Nancy Adler, a professor at McGill University in Montreal. She has found that women expatriates feel that their femaleness is an advantage. They say that because of their uniqueness they are highly visible, which is important if you are in an industry with close client contact. In addition, these women feel that, in comparison with their male colleagues, they have better access to clients, who are curious to meet them because often they have never worked with a woman before. As a result, women find it easier to get appointments, they are often given longer appointments, and they therefore get more information from their clients. Consequently, they are remembered when they call again.

Many businessmen have failed in their attempts to do business in many parts of the world because they have used the push style of negotiating instead of the pull style. Push includes persuading by using logic, debates, facts, and proposals. This style also includes asserting or applying pressure by telling the clients what they want, what's in it for them, or what will happen if they don't agree.

Because these (mostly male) executives use styles of negotiating that are so unsuited to countries overseas, they rarely get the chance to make their sales pitch. But even if they are patient enough to have the opportunity to make a presentation, the push style probably won't succeed anyway. It is simply out of sync with the tempo of business in many parts of the world. The push style of negotiating overseas leaves little room for uncertainty. The major reason that it doesn't work in a foreign atmosphere is that a decision is always forced by this style. It draws to a yes/no conclusion with little of the ambiguity that is so necessary in dealing successfully overseas.

Another error often made is to try to close the deal at the first meeting. This makes many overseas clients wary because a trusting relationship has not yet been developed. The traditional U.S. salesman would not want to make more trips, nor would his management want him to. But this shortsightedness is much more costly in the long run. What sales and management need to understand is that to do volume business over the long term requires an investment of time in the short term.

One of the successful negotiator's biggest tasks is. to educate management in the home office about the differences in time required to bring the deal to completion. Few deals are closed on the first meeting anywhere in the world. Repeat visits always have to be scheduled. Even if, in a rare case, a deal is concluded on the first visit, after-sales relationships must be cultivated. When a deal is closed, the successful negotiator does not pack and run. She invites the client to a dinner where they will celebrate their agreement, for in the successful deal everyone is a winner.

Future meetings in the client's country or in the United States should be suggested and planned for. A great amount of time must be spent; however, a business friend made overseas is not just a source of increased or repeat purchases, but a means to open doors to a vast market.

In a recent study done at a leading business school, 41 men and 23 women were videotaped in a simulated negotiation situation. The findings concluded that when a man visualizes a negotiation situation he sees it as a one-shot deal to win or lose, like a sport or game. A women sees it as part of a long-term relationship. This shows again that women are better suited for international negotiating than most men.

The interlocking relationships in business overseas are so complex and circuitous that one small successful deal can lead to introductions to previously impenetrable markets. For the same reasons, the loss of a deal due to insensitivity toward one foreign client may seriously hurt your chances of closing a deal with other companies in that country.

Almost all successful international negotiators share the following traits: They ask questions and reveal feelings (without sounding naive); they use few reasons to back up arguments; they check often to make sure they are understood; they avoid irritating, confrontative statements, counterproposals, and defend/attack stances; and they label speech ("If I could make a suggestion..."). In many cultures, directness is not appreciated, and can even be interpreted as abrupt and hostile.

Some of these same characteristics are considered ineffective in business meetings in the United States, but they are precisely the attributes for successful negotiating in most countries overseas. While men in the United States typically grab the floor by interrupting another speaker, women have been conditioned from childhood to believe that it is impolite to interrupt, and will wait for a turn to speak. In U.S. business, when a women does speak up she may undermine her credibility by using tentative phrases such as "I think," by turning statements into questions, or by making indirect statements. A woman may say, "Maybe we should send the widget" or "Don't you think we should send them the widget?" instead of "Let's send them the widget." This lack of being presumptuous, while considered a weakness in the United States, is an asset in doing business overseas.

The successful negotiator knows more than the proper style of international business negotiating. She also knows how to use this style in a cultural context. Small things like giving sizes, weights, and distances in the metric system, and temperatures in the celsius and not fahrenheit scale; knowing that the words billion and trillion refer to different numbers in some countries than they do in the United States, and so forth, are contributions you can make to change the image of the ethnocentric American.

It is important to begin the process of negotiation before you leave the United States, through correspondence, telexes, and telephone calls. For Japan and other parts of the Far East, and for the Middle East and Latin America, a better way of beginning a business relationship may be to contact the U.S. representative of your client's company if it is large enough to have a U.S. office. For smaller companies, a trade association, social organization, government agency, or bank in the United States could be contacted for introductions. Try the Arab-American Chamber of Commerce, Latin American Chamber of Commerce, Japan Trade Center, European American Bank, or the commercial attaché in the country's embassy or consulate. Through these resources you may be able to meet an influential or informative person who can provide introductions for you.

If you have written letters and have not been answered, don't assume a complete lack of interest. Your reply may not be forthcoming if the client has limited ability in English, needs more time to think about your offer, or needs more information about your company. Send another letter with supporting information about you and your company. Do not become impatient or feel insulted if a month elapses before you receive a reply. Continue finding ways to explain your purpose. Show knowledge and understanding of the country's history, culture, and business practices (even in a letter). Make references that show your expertise in your product or business area. If you receive a reply that shows even the slightest interest, make plans for a face-to-face meeting. Again, in most countries business will not progress further until and unless this meeting take place. When it does, be prepared for a little surprise on your client's part at his first sight of you, even if he already knows your're a woman and is happy to deal with you.

In preparing for your meeting there are certain universal rules to follow: Learn something about the political, historical, cultural, and business background of the country. Know the company with which you are dealing (the international edition of Dun and Bradstreet or company tear sheets ordered from D&B are a worthwhile investment). Be able to speak at least a few words of the client's language; if you are reasonably fluent, so much the better. Know your product or service completely, and be able to answer all questions concerning what you are selling or negotiating. Consider your efforts an investment; the contract or deal you negotiate will take some time, but your rewards will be for the long term.

Make sure you bring an adequate supply of business cards. If working in Japan and China, have them printed in Japanese or Chinese on the other side. If you run short of cards you can have them printed on fairly short notice in almost any country. Your business card is even more important overseas than in the United States. It is extremely important in Japan, where there is an etiquette of ways to present and receive cards. In all countries you should stand up when presenting and receiving cards. When you receive a card, read it carefully and either keep it in front of you or put it away. If you put it away, make sure you know the person's name so you don't fumble in your pocket to look at the card. In all countries offer a firm handshake; in Japan, add a slight bow.

In almost every overseas business encounter, you shouldn't expect to conclude substantive matters during the first meeting. This meeting is a getting-to-know-you exercise. The further away you get from Western Europe, the more your client will want to know about you and your company. Allow some time for your client to get used to you, the executive woman. It is not likely that he (or his company) will have done a great deal of business with U.S. women previously, so this is your opportunity to show your professionalism, ability, sophistication, calm, and wit—in short, all the things in which women excel.

If you have been made to wait for your appointment for what seems like an inordinate amount of time, do not feel insulted. Understand that other nationalities, especially Arabs or Latin Americans, do not experience time in the same way that people in the United States do. Don't assume you are being discriminated against because you are a woman. Above all, do not refer to the amount of time you have been waiting, as it will make it obvious that you are irritated or insulted and give your client an upper hand in negotiations. Time has less priority in certain countries throughout the world. Similarly, in Japan meetings are usually held on time, but negotiations can be subject to endless delays due to the Japanese style of decision making.

Your initial meeting should revolve around mutual acquaintances, discussions about each other's country (here, it is always useful to have read a book by an esteemed author, seen a victory by the country's soccer team, heard some music of the country, or have some similar experience to discuss), and suggestions for future meetings. This might be the time to invite your client and his associates to drinks or dinner. While your client will feel he is in control of the meeting, it is you who will in fact be controlling the situation. If your client does not feel threatened or rushed, as he might if he were negotiating with a U.S. businessman, your dealings will be easier.

If your first meeting is held at lunch or dinner, keep in mind that in most countries it is not polite to discuss business while eating. In the Middle East and India, do not use your left hand while eating unless you are taken to a Western-style restaurant and presented with a knife and fork. You will probably not be served alcohol in Moslem countries; if it doesn't appear, don't ask for it.

In most (non-Moslem) societies a toast is always appropriate, preferably with the local wine or spirit. Watch out for other cultural norms with which you may not be familiar. For example, in Japan it is considered rude to blow your nose loudly in public, but don't be surprised to see people picking their noses.

Another cultural factor to be aware of is the concept of space. Americans conduct business at a distance of about two to three feet, but overseas, particularly in Latin America, the Middle East, and India, conversations are held at very close proximity. Recognizing this is particularly important for women. If your client stands three inches away from you, this does not mean that he is making sexual overtures, and it is most important to avoid taking a step back to increase the distance between you and him. This is perceived in Latin America and the Middle East as the proof of the U.S. coldness that they have heard about. In Great Britain, Germany, Switzerland, and parts of Scandinavia, cultural norms are somewhat similar to those in the United States, but in all other places, know your client's differences and be sensitive to them.

All your preliminary discussions are a part of the negotiating process. In many places, if the preliminaries are not to the client's liking and he feels that a real relationship is not beginning, there will be no further negotiations. During these preliminaries it is a good idea to avoid discussing religion and politics.

In the Middle East, everything is dictated by religion, and a negotiation may be stopped to allow for the prayers that are called for five times every day. Since most of Latin America has moved toward democracy, the subject of politics is not quite as volatile as it once was. Acknowledge the new leaders and progress, but avoid opinions on ideology.

There are a number of European countries where the young population is becoming increasingly anti-American. Germany, for instance, has a highly militant group that resents the United States for its nuclear proliferation. Other countries such as France, Greece, Spain, and Italy have strong socialist parties and are at times critical of the United States. Avoid falling into traps of agreeing (no matter what your feelings) or disagreeing. Try skillfully to change the subject.

Before you sit down to bargain be sure to define your own goals. Try to understand the client's objectives beforehand. Since price and quality are not the only important factors in a deal overseas, learn what alternate currencies can be offered to sweeten a deal. These may be in the form of a longer warranty, an option added at no extra charge, a relative considered for employment, a stock option, or any perks that may increase the attractiveness of the deal.

When you finally progress to the negotiating stage of your relationship, be sure you are aware of the business characteristics of that country.

Gift Giving in Different Cultures

Small gifts are appropriate in any business negotiation anywhere in the world. Items such as pens, pen sets, key rings, small tools, cups, flashlights, and the like, engraved with your company's logo, are not only appreciated but virtually essential. These gifts are more advertisements and mementos than true gifts, and should be considered as part of the advertising budget.

In many countries where you need to develop a long-term personal relationship in order to do business, larger gifts may be appropriate. In Latin America, a good bottle of scotch and U.S. cigarettes (especially Marlboro) are much appreciated. Recently, scotch and U.S. cigarettes have also seemed to be the gift of choice for clients in the Peoples' Republic of China.

While alcohol is prohibited in most of the Moslem Middle East, cigarettes are not, and your Arab and Israeli clients alike will appreciate U.S. brands. The Russians too are changing their attitudes toward drinking, so chocolates or nuts are a safer bet to bring to the Soviet Union. In most European countries, entertainment in the form of dinner at a good restaurant or tickets to the ballet, an opera, or a concert are preferred gifts. Of course, if you know your client's family quite well it is also appropriate to give a gift to the children in the form of a U.S.-made toy or game.

In Japan, gift giving is an important part of the culture. One of the gift giving seasons begins July 15 and lasts for a month. This is timed to the summer salary bonus that is standard in Japan. If you are negotiating during this period, you should present a gift to your client and be prepared to receive gifts in return. Glassware, food, alcohol, and designer items are highly desired. Of course, if you are in the midst of negotiating in a country where Christmas is celebrated, gifts are again in order.

Be aware, however, that there are certain gifts that may be totally inappropriate in some parts of the world. Cheese is not eaten in China, where it is considered to be spoiled milk, and your Chinese client would be upset to receive it. Clocks are also objectionable in China because the word for clock is similar to a word associated with a death ritual. Linen handkerchiefs are associated with sadness in Brazil, and knives may indicate cutting off a relationship in many parts of Latin America. Avoid sending chrysanthemums in Italy, where they're associated with mourning.

Indeed, in Europe, you should also be careful not only of *which* flowers to bring as gifts, but *how many*. In Germany, never send a dozen flowers to your host or client, as Germans are familiar with the expression "cheaper by the dozen." Throughout Europe, you should always send an uneven number of flowers, but not 13, because many Europeans still associate the number 13 with bad luck.

In most of Europe and in Japan, U.S. jazz records are extremely desirable gifts. In France, West Germany, and Scandinavia especially, a large number of people are jazz enthusiasts and consider U.S. jazz to be the only acceptable form of that music. In Japan, U.S. jazz and rock-and-roll records are sought after.

Large gifts, on the other hand, are not usually appropriate to give or to accept. An expensive item given or accepted may be considered a bribe, and may often put you in a compromising situation, ethically or legally. It is best to know the laws and attitudes concerning bribery, giving gifts of high value, and making large donations to charities in the country in which you negotiate. Giving gifts of high value is generally condemned in the United States, but in many countries gift giving on a somewhat higher price level is acceptable or even the rule.

While giving a gift as part of the price for the awarding of a contract or closing of a deal may not be illegal, U.S. business executives may have some ethical reservations. As an alternative, if a donation to a legitimate local charity greatly increases your chances of closing a deal, it should be considered as part of the cost of doing business.

How can you determine when giving or accepting a gift becomes a bribe? Intent is one way to determine the difference. If you or your client perceive that a gift is simply an excuse to improperly influence the other, then it is obviously a bribe. Secrecy is another indicator of an inappropriate inducement. In many Arab countries, gift giving is done in public so that the giver's generosity will earn him respect. If a large gift is clandestinely offered or received, you may be running into trouble. For example, a U.S. executive was traveling in Saudi Arabia and received a paper sack while boarding the plane back to the United States. The negotiations were not yet complete and his Saudi client was still seeking concessions from the U.S. company. Opening the bag on the plane and expecting to find a snack, the executive discovered instead a half dozen expensive watches. Recognizing this as an attempt at bribery, the executive returned them. However, gift giving is a private affair in many Asian countries, and a privately given gift would not necessarily be considered bribery there.

Large gifts may often involve a breach of law or ethics. While a large gift to the owner of a privately owned business overseas or a donation to his favorite charity is probably not illegal, a large gift to a purchasing agent for the purpose of influencing his judgment on behalf of his company is unethical, and, in some places, illegal. (For example, many U.S. states and some foreign countries have laws prohibiting commercial bribery.) Even if not illegal, it is often bad business ethics.

Bribery of foreign government officials by U.S. businesses may be in direct violation of the U.S. Foreign Corrupt Practices Act of 1977. While bribery is accepted and acceptable in some countries, especially those with low-level, poorly paid functionaries, high-level bribery is not. For example, if you want your shipment of perishables to be inspected before they rot, it is wise in many countries to attach a five- or ten-dollar bill to the invoice or bill of lading. This is considered greasing the wheels of commerce, and is regularly accepted. To influence a choice between equals (your company versus another company closing a deal), giving a U.S.-made small appliance or other moderately priced gift is also usually acceptable. However, giving a large gift to secure a deal to which your company is not entitled is improper. For example, a large sum of money given to an official for exclusive purchase of your disinfecting chemicals, whether they are competitive or not, would be considered an illegal bribe.

In some places, most notably Mexico and Italy, commercial and individual bribery is a way of life. Be certain to research what is and isn't acceptable, and be careful of running afoul of the local laws as well as U.S. statutes. In these cases especially it is helpful to have a local contact advise you of standard practice. If that is impossible, do as much research as you can on the local customs and practices before you begin your negotiations.

A Word about the Foreign Corrupt Practices Act

In 1977, upset about political scandals caused in some foreign countries where top government officials were found to have accepted bribes from U.S.-based multinational corporations, Congress unanimously passed the Foreign Corrupt Practices Act (FCPA).

The major provision of the FCPA prohibits any U.S.-based company from "corruptly" giving or offering money or "anything of value" to a foreign political official "for the purpose of obtaining or retaining business." The requirement that the payment be "corrupt" excludes "grease payments" such as small tips to low-level government clerks for routine approval of export documents. To be illegal under the FCPA, the payment must be made to a foreign government official or to an official of a foreign political party. But in many parts of the world, where industries are state-run or where governmental "consultants" act as go-betweens on business deals, the application of the FCPA to ordinary business deals can be quite broad. Bribes are illegal even if paid indirectly, such as when a U.S. company reimburses the "expenses" of a foreign subsidiary or a local distributor, knowing that some of the money will be used for bribes. The FCPA carries severe criminal penalties, including large fines (up to one million dollars for corporations) and jail sentences of up to five years.

Other provisions of the FCPA require U.S. companies to adopt accounting practices that will enable top management to be aware of any bribery being carried on by low-level sales people or foreign subsidiaries. Many provisions of the FCPA are quite technical, such as rules specifying what percentage of stock a U.S. parent must own in a foreign subsidiary before it will be held responsible for the subsidiary's actions. Other terms in the law are vague, such as the prohibition on payments made "corruptly." Here, as with any situation on the border between innocent gift giving and illegal bribery, your wisest course is to check with the legal department at the home office before making a payment that might later be questioned.

In 1988, Congress amended the FCPA after hearing many complaints that the law unrealistically limited U.S. competitiveness in the export market. The 1988 amendments made it clear that grease payments for routine governmental services are legal, as are routine promotional gifts, reimbursement of reasonable expenses for promotional meals or travel, and payments that are legal under the laws of the foreign country.

Even as amended, however, the FCPA is still ambiguous in many ways. The Reagan and Bush administrations have not enforced the law very actively, however. Still, the law remains on the books, and caution is advisable.

5

Doing Business in the World Marketplace: Asia, the Far East, and Down Under

Japan

Despite the complaints by many U.S. companies about Japanese protectionism, you *can* do business with Japan if you have the patience and know-how. In Japan you will probably have to start your negotiation with a middle manager. At this level you should be as detached and technically accurate as possible. You will then speak with the general manager or a director who is a step higher in rank. He will want to hear about your firm's background and reliability. He will also want to know something about you and your experience. While in recent years U.S. businesswomen have been doing business with Japan, the Japanese are still not comfortable with women in positions of power.

Japan is, after all, still one of the most macho cultures in the world. However, a new breed of Japanese women are beginning to assert themselves. In 1989, after the Japanese government had been wracked by sex and corruption scandals, the women's vote for the first time had a major impact on the election results. Women have now begun to hold a few major positions in the upper ranks of Japanese politics.

At all meetings, speaking even a few words of Japanese is greatly appreciated. With the introduction of each person, be sure to present your business card so that it is facing the client and not upside down. Have your business cards printed in English on one side and in Japanese on the other. Hand your card to the most important person first.

Most features of Japanese etiquette and behavior are contrary to what you're accustomed to. You must *never* blow your nose in public under any circumstances. This is considered disgusting—even though you may see your Japanese client or host openly sticking a finger into his nose! If you're invited to a restaurant or private home, be sure to take off your shoes and use the slippers provided for you. At lunch, if you order the popular noodle soup, it's considered excellent manners to make a lot of noise slurping up the noodles.

Whatever your proposal, make sure that you can support it with facts. Many Japanese executives are so much better informed about the West than we are about Japan that you must be sure of your facts. When business talks are in the initial stages in Japan, your Japanese client will be sizing you up. It is not until your negotiation has progressed to a very serious level (if it does) that your Japanese counterpart will reveal what he really feels about your proposition.

Always speak clearly but softly, and use only standard English. Unless your client speaks fluent English or you speak fluent Japanese, use an interpreter who has been recommended. The added advantage of interpreters is that they can modify your direct talk to conform with the Japanese way of thinking. In Japanese, the communication style depends on who is talking to whom. There are many levels of honorifics (deferential titles) and many levels of politeness. Always remember that in Japan, it is important to sell yourself before you can sell your product or service.

The progress of negotiating the deal may be frustrating, because it seems much slower than in countries such as the United States. Don't let your exasperation show. Try to keep a slight smile on your face or show no emotion at all.

Your client may appear to be avoiding a direct answer to your offers. Often, the Japanese have difficulty saying "no" to any part of your proposal, even if they do not agree at all. This results from the wish of the Japanese to present at least an appearance of harmony. Remember that *hai,* the Japanese word for "yes," doesn't always mean agreement; it oftens means only "Yes, I understand what you are saying." A direct "no" is considered rude. The Japanese way is to talk around a subject for so long and in so many ways that everyone understands the others' point of view. No one loses face because no one has to back down. If you're confused whether your clients are really in agreement, ask directly but respectfully for their opinion, explaining that you would be grateful to have it expressed to avoid any misunderstandings later.

Sometimes during a meeting in Japan your client will interrupt the negotiation to call for tea. This utilizes a style of negotiating known as disengaging. When tension is high or the negotiator wants time to think, disengaging provides temporary relief. You may also want to use the tactic of disengaging at some point in the negotiating process (not only in Japan, but anywhere in the world) by asking for a glass of water to give yourself an opportunity to recoup or to refocus your proposal.

At times during an impasse in the discussion, your Japanese client will remain silent. At other times your client may not even respond to a question. Do not become uneasy or make clarifying statements. This is where many U.S. businessmen voluntarily give in on a disputed point or say something they shouldn't just to get the conversation started. These few minutes of silence are only another form of disengaging, not an example of manipulative or shrewd behavior on your client's part. Silence is their way of stepping back and pondering the question.

The group decision-making process is still common in Japan. This is one of the reasons that negotiating is so time-consuming. The final decision is based on a consensus of many individuals. It may take a long time, and you will have to participate in endless meetings. However, when the decision is finally made, implementation of the program will quickly follow.

Although great patience is necessary when negotiating a deal anywhere in Japan, this is especially true in Tokyo. In Osaka, Japan's second city, you will find the people slightly more direct and outspoken. Osaka's strong business orientation makes negotiating seem more Western in style, but you should still be careful to observe all Japanese customs.

At the same time that the Japanese management style is becoming popular in the United States, the Japanese are beginning to admire the style of management they think of as American. A 1985 *Fortune* article reported that a leading Japanese paper had published a list of the best-run companies in Japan and had given the first and second places to companies that were run autocratically or as a "one-man show." These aggressively run companies could be prototypes of Japanese competitors in a quickly changing world.

Do not forget Japan's endless fascination with the United States.

The Japanese are just as mystified by and interested in us as we are in them. There is constant imitation of each other's customs and innovations. This is fertile ground for profitable business dealings.

China

Negotiating a deal in the People's Republic of China is one of the biggest business challenges you may ever face. This market, of more than one billion people, has just recently been opened to foreign trade. In some ways, China is totally unique, unlike any business culture you will ever encounter. However, certain features of the Chinese business culture are very similar to those of Japan, including lengthy negotiations, the concept of saving face, and the importance of presenting business cards. In fact, you will find these similarities in other parts of Asia: in Taiwan and Korea particularly, and in Hong Kong, Singapore, Malaysia, Thailand, and Indonesia to varying degrees.

The Chinese have very strong incentives to attract foreign ventures. One reason is that they have over four hundred thousand old factories to renovate. The two dozen foreign investment laws passed in recent years to ensure the legal protection of these ventures indicates the Chinese commitment to foreign trade. Special economic zones have been created to absorb foreign technology and disseminate Western techniques. Inside these zones a free market system is being established. Although the Chinese press may deny it, the zones are enclaves of capitalism within China.

China has also begun a major effort to expand its trade with the United States. Total U.S.-Chinese trade (imports and exports) was over five billion dollars in 1988. Although many U.S. and other foreign firms put their plans for joint ventures and increased trade with China on hold after the bloody suppression of student demonstrations in 1989, Chinese officials are actively trying to woo their foreign trading partners back. It remains to be seen, however, whether the political crackdown of 1989 will lead to a return to more rigidly socialist economic policies. There is also some risk of further political instability. It seems most likely, however, that U.S.-Chinese trade will continue to increase.

You and your group (the Chinese prefer to deal with a group rather than a single negotiator) will probably be greeted at the airport by a welcoming party and sent off to your hotel. When you meet your Chinese client, offer your business cards, which should be printed in Chinese on the reverse side. Here, as in any culture that respects age, you should express the hope that your client (who is likely to be much older than you) is in good health. When beginning your meetings, be prepared for lengthy negotiations. Negotiations with Chinese ministries or corporations over the simplest contracts may take months, with many visits needed and delays occurring frequently. The Chinese bureaucracy still has a built-in inertia at the middle-management level. Your constant, patient attention will be required to ensure progress on a deal.

The more advance information you can give your Chinese client about what you hope to accomplish in China, the likelier you are to be pleased at the results. The Chinese do not like surprises in their business dealings with Americans; they prefer to know exactly what issues will be raised so they can have responses planned ahead of time. Early information allows them to line up the most appropriate participants on their side so that you will be more likely to talk to the proper counterpart.

When your Chinese clients enter a room, they generally do so in protocol order, with the highest-ranking person coming in first. The exception is the interpreter, who will stand next to the delegation leader in order to provide him with a voice. The Chinese will also assume that the first member of your negotiating team is head of your group. You can avoid the confusion of having a recording secretary taken for the CEO by observing the Chinese protocols. Your client may occasionally have a woman in the negotiating team, as one of the principles of the Chinese communist system is to promote sexual equality. After you are introduced and cards are exchanged, be sure to address your client correctly. The Chinese put their surname first and proper name last; the given name is rarely used in conversation.

Meetings in China always begin on time, but small talk and politeness are exchanged before any serious discussion. As in Japan, it is considered impolite to get down to business immediately. Discussions of the weather, your stay in China, and the other cities in China you have visited are good ways to break the ice. Internal politics or foreign policies are not suitable subjects for discussion. You shouldn't mention Taiwan even if you have recently been there on business or pleasure. Don't bring up the growth that China has experienced, as your client will be well aware of the many problems still facing the country.

When you finally get the signal to begin discussing business, you should pause frequently so that the interpreter can digest and translate your remarks. There is a very wide cultural gulf to be bridged because China has been isolated for so long. As in Japan, if your client seems to sidestep direct questions, it is either because he or she doesn't know the answer or because the answer is no, which is considered impolite to say. If you get an indication that your client needs to check on something before giving an answer, ask him to designate the contact person with whom you may follow up later. This will help speed the negotiating process.

Be aware that your client may try to pressure you to make concessions. He may try to convince you that other companies are interested in the same contract. If other firms are in the running, your client may exaggerate the concessions that those companies have been willing to make. Don't be pressured into giving the store away. Instead of making concessions try to negotiate with alternate inducements such as warranties, after-sale consulting, or other perks. As a courtesy to your client, have copies of your proposals translated into Chinese so that lower-ranking officials can study them.

Either you or your client can end a meeting. The ranking member of either group can comment on how much of the client's time he or she has already taken up, and politely request that another meeting be scheduled.

Even more so than in Japan, the negotiating process in China is an art that requires great skill and patience. As there is virtually no private sector in China, everything is controlled by the government and you cannot do business in China without the support of an official body. Just getting the OK to do business in China can take time, and much more time will be taken up by the actual negotiating process when you do get the go-ahead. But negotiating in China may be well worth your patience. While waiting three years for the first order to go through or to secure the joint venture may seem inordinate, the Chinese market is well worth the trouble because brand loyalty is very strong in China.

For the Chinese, the concept of trust is an important part of deciding to whom to award the contract. Before a contract is awarded or a deal made, the Chinese have to come to respect you as an individual. The process they use to determine your sincerity often includes a banquet. While it is important not to make serious social mistakes at these ceremonies, minor gaffes are not critical. You can politely refuse the sea slugs without losing the deal. Your attitude is what counts. Your usual sensitivity, caution, and careful observation of others' behavior will ensure your success. Toasting your host with alcohol or another beverage is customary. Conversation need not be complicated; in fact, you are best off sticking to a discussion of the excellent food, or the Chinese language, climate, and geography. Be careful about putting anyone on the spot by asking questions. Embarrassments are considered a serious breach of etiquette. Do not attempt to become personally friendly with anyone in your client's group, as China does not encourage individual friendships between foreigners and Chinese citizens. *Friendship* refers to cooperation and good working relationships between your company and the Chinese group. Toast the friendship of your company with China, enjoy the food, and, as always, be patient.

Patience paid off for Barbara R. Pick, executive vice president of General Robotics Corporation, a Hartford, Wisconsin, manufacturer of computer parts and systems. After 20 weeks in China and three different trips, Pick in 1983 secured two major contracts for her company totalling eight million dollars—thus more than doubling company sales.

Taiwan

The Far East is the fastest growing industrial area in the world, and U.S. business travelers are spending a tremendous amount of time there. Negotiations may be long and tedious, but the results can be spectacular.

Tawian is a fast-growing, aggressive economy located only 90 miles off the Chinese mainland. Taiwan is light years away from China in its capitalist economy, and has industrialized so rapidly that its infrastructure hasn't caught up. The Taiwanese do a great deal of business with the United States, and Taiwan is an excellent market for U.S. goods and services. In fact, the United States exports more goods to Taiwan than to Italy. The Taiwanese like and admire Americans. The people are ethnically Chinese, but many have been educated in the United States, making Taiwan an interesting amalgam of old-fashioned Chinese sensibilities and modern Western ideas. You should remember, when doing business in Taiwan, not to mention mainland China or local politics, even though the government has been liberalizing its policies over the past few years.

Despite the vast political and economic differences, many of the same customs are observed in Taiwan as in China, although within a more relaxed atmosphere. Once again, be sure to have your business cards printed in Chinese on the reverse side, and prepare for your negotiation in a manner similar to that in China. The banquet is an important part of a business relationship. Observe the same protocols as in China. In addition, you should bring small gifts to your client.

Negotiations cannot be rushed, but there is a great desire on the part of young Taiwanese to continue the country's development at a rapid pace. You may find negotiations moving more quickly than you anticipate, but you should never be the one to hurry things along.

Korea

Korea is, in its rapid development, somewhat similar to Taiwan, and in some ways has also been compared favorably to Japan in its aggressive growth. Korea's "Big Four" companies—Daewoo, Hyundai, Samsung, and Gold Star—are becoming as much household names in the United States as Sony and Toyota. However, it is wise not to make any comparisons between Korea and Japan, as Koreans are sensitive about the dominance of Japanese business in the region. The Koreans are outgoing and somewhat less formal than the Japanese or Chinese. However, the concept of face is equally important to Koreans. Age, position in society or business, and education are highly respected in Korea.

Koreans are very sensitive to the division of the country into communist North Korea and capitalist South Korea. Tensions between the North and South have eased somewhat lately, and South Korea held its first democratic presidential elections in 1987 after years of authoritarian rule. Nonetheless, it is unwise to discuss anything having to do with local or international politics. The best topic of discussion is the exponential growth rate achieved by Korea over the last 20 years.

The majority of the population shares only three family names: Kim, Park, and Lee. It will be easier for you to use titles such as Manager Lee and Director Kim to avoid confusion among similarly named members of the delegation.

Even though English is widely spoken in Korea, it is a good idea to use an interpreter, especially if you are negotiating a very sensitive or expensive deal.

Koreans can sometimes seem very direct in their questions; however, it is not a sign of rudeness, it is simply a sign of interest. Conversely, formal manners and behavior are very important in negotiating until a relationship of trust has been established.

Singapore

Singapore is a physically attractive, rapidly developing island nation made up of 75 percent ethnic Chinese, and minorities of Malays,

Indians, and Eurasians. Many of the young, wealthy Singaporeans study in European and U.S. universities, and have rapidly accelerated the pace of doing business. Women are often highly educated and work in the arts and professions.

Be punctual at your meetings, as being late is considered rude. Good opening topics of conversation are places you have visited and the beauty of Singapore. Avoid any religious or political comments. Singapore is a very modern Asian country and quite Western-looking. English is spoken widely and most people are bilingual.

Do not try to get to know your Singaporean client in a hurry. Wait until you have met the client a few times before inviting him or her to dinner. Do not invite public-sector or government officials to dinner as they are not permitted to accept. Interestingly, once you have established a relationship with your client, you can even discuss business over a formal dinner.

Hong Kong

Hong Kong is a British Colony with a 98 percent Chinese population. English is the official language and business is conducted in English. Hong Kong is a strange blend of Asian and European cultures with a totally international demeanor. It is a center for international banking and finance, with a high-pressure business environment. With growth have come all the irritants of modern society. Hong Kong has one of the more corrupt business systems in the world. In the last 10 years or so, this corruption has come under close scrutiny of the Hong Kong government, but has proven hard to eradicate.

In 1997, Great Britain is scheduled to return Hong Kong to mainland Chinese rule. China has promised to maintain Hong Kong's capitalist system and democratic freedoms for 50 years, but many locals are skeptical—especially after the 1989 upheaval in China—and some are fleeing the country. At this time, however, Hong Kong still remains one of the easiest places in Asia for an American to do business.

When doing business in Hong Kong, be careful and get to know your client as well as possible. Here again the concept of face must be respected. The obligatory banquet is an integral part of the negotiations.

Hong Kong's attitude toward women in business is not totally liberated yet, but it is the best in the Pacific Rim. The vast amount of U.S. business done with Hong Kong is bringing women onto negotiating teams, and the close business relationship with mainland China's more egalitarian society has also had a positive effect on the climate for women.

The negotiating process is slow in Hong Kong. As in any country with a history of corruption, caution is necessary. If you are going to Hong Kong to establish a link with mainland China, be sure that your contact is legitimate.

You should also be aware of the practice of *fung shui*, a popular form of occultism. The best times and circumstances for beginning negotiations may be determined by a *fung shui* expert. If your client proposes such a ritual, do not ridicule it; respect it and then get on with business.

Southeast Asia

Thailand and Indonesia are two developing nations in Southeast Asia. The Moslem religion predominates in Indonesia, and the Buddhist faith in Thailand. Your sensitivity to the customs and laws involved is an absolute requirement to doing business in these countries. Both countries are quite poor, and the pace of negotiations is extremely frustrating and slow. While you may encounter some difficulty as a foreign woman in a Moslem society, there are no major legal restrictions against women doing business in Indonesia. In fact, in both countries there are some women in senior positions, particularly in privately owned businesses.

Negotiating in Malaysia may pose some problems for women. Approximately 45 percent of the population is Moslem, with Chinese and Indian minorities. However, the Chinese dominate the business community and you will most likely be dealing with them. Avoid any discussion of religion, as it is a very sensitive issue. Although politics can be discussed, better yet would be conversations about family, sports, or travel. Comments on the success of the client are always appreciated. Carefully avoid comparisons between the West and Malaysia. The concept of face must be respected. However, Malaysians are not generally as diplomatic in their dealings as other Southeast Asians.

Your client will be polite and attentive but occasionally suspicious. He will ask you many questions and answer as few questions as he can. Entertainment is an important part of business in Malaysia, and you should invite your client to lunch or dinner to follow up on your meeting. Invite all persons involved in the negotiations to join you.

In your negotiations do act humbly and be aware of the Malaysian sensibilities. They are shrewd businessmen and may know a good deal more than they let on.

The Philippines is a developing country, formerly a colony of the United States and, before that, of Spain. Most of the population is Catholic, and the democratically elected government is run by a woman, Corazón Aquino. The United States is popular, and English is widely spoken although Tagalog (Filipino) is the official language. Spanish is also spoken, and many of your clients will have Spanish names.

Australia and New Zealand

Australia is a very different type of market in this region. Seeming to be cross between the United States, the United Kingdom, and Canada, Australia is not exactly like any of these countries. Australians are unique, resourceful, friendly, and energetic people, and dislike being told how to do things. In your negotiations be honest and forthcoming, as Australians regard extreme formality as insincere and artificial. Be careful to avoid comparisons between Australians and the United States or the United Kingdom. For all their geographical isolation, this Western nation is technologically progressive and very sophisticated.

New Zealand, a British Dominion 1,100 miles southeast of Australia, is quite similar in its culture to Australia. New Zealanders, however, are very proud of their autonomy, and will strongly resent any comparison to their larger neighbor.

You should be extremely punctual for any meeting in New Zealand; your clients will probably arrive five minutes early, and will expect you to do the same. New Zealanders are very sensitive to issues of race, so this topic should be avoided in all conversations. The weather and sports are good subjects of conversations. Informality is the rule in business in New Zealand and Australia. New Zealanders and Australians resent heavy-handed superiors or toadying subordinates, and work with few rigid lines of authority. Your easygoing U.S. attitudes will get you far down under!

6

Doing Business in the World Marketplace: Europe 1992 and Beyond

You will find that Europe is the most familiar climate in which to negotiate, but don't be lulled into thinking that Europe is an easy place in which to do business or that negotiation styles are the same throughout Europe. If your travel experience in Europe have been limited to vacationing in a city or resort, be prepared for very different attitudes on the part of the Europeans in business situations.

Many Europeans speak English in addition to their own language. It is not unusual for a European to speak two or three other languages—and well. The countries of Europe are mostly quite small geographically, and most border on several other nations. This proximity provides for a good deal of cultural intermingling and intra-European business. However, each country is very different from the other in history, politics, and economics, and in the national personality and attitude. There are often vast differences even within one country. For example, in many ways Northern Italy is much more like Switzerland than like Southern Italy.

There are, however, some generalities found throughout Europe. Despite some recent change, the old social structure still dominates throughout Western Europe. Society is stratified by family tradition, and most working-class people do not become educated past high school. University education is still primarily for the upper classes. Most Europeans still disdain the concept of business; it is far more acceptable to become educated as a professional. Doctors, lawyers, engineers, and professors are more respected than business executives. You will, however, find many people in business who were trained in the professions. The business school curriculum as we know it in the United States is rare, and few Europeans want the title Master of Business Administration. Business executives may use their previous professional titles such as Doctor or Lawyer.

Business in Europe is not nearly the all-consuming passion it is in the United States. While in many countries, notably Germany and Austria, work is taken very seriously, even in those countries business is not the primary focus of life. People work hard and put in long hours but are somewhat less driven than Americans. In most of Europe, the tradition of gathering in cafes, traveling, reading, and relaxing are as important as working hard. Almost everyone in Europe gets a month's vacation annually, whereas in the United States it may take years to earn that much vacation time.

As in Asia, Europeans highly prize experienced people rather than young go-getters. A newly minted MBA from a top school without any experience can earn fantastic sums of money in the United States, but Europeans are not very impressed with this credential. Europeans are fairly risk-averse, and most of them prefer a modest but secure position rather than a chancy, exciting opportunity.

European thrift and economy are remarkable, particularly in Germany, Switzerland, and Belgium. People there will repair rather than throw away, save rather than spend, and in general make do. These are characteristics of two-thousand-year-old cultures, as opposed to the two-hundred-year-old culture of the United States. Consequently, change is somewhat slower in Europe. While there are many women who work, there are fewer women who are career professionals than in the United States. Female executives on the middle- and upper-management levels are few, but their numbers are beginning to grow. Recently, a number of lawsuits by European women seeking equal pay for equal jobs have begun to make headlines.

It is evident that many U.S. techniques are being adopted into European business practice. While the fast-track, pressured atmosphere of the United States has not yet been imported, certain U.S. marketing and advertising concepts have been successfully transplanted to Europe.

Europe 1992

In 1992 the 12 countries of the European Community (Great Britain, Ireland, Portugal, Spain, France, the Netherlands, Luxembourg, Belgium, Denmark, West Germany, Italy, and Greece) will break down all internal trade barriers. This "United Europe" will consist of over 320 million consumers with buying power of over four trillion dollars—a market almost as large as the United States and Japan combined. For the U.S. businesswoman, Europe now provides opportunities equal to those of the Pacific Rim. For the Europeans, this consolidation represents a reawakening after decades of losing economic prominence to the United States and Japan. As Carlo De Benedetti, CEO of Italy's Olivetti and Co., put it, "For Europe, 1992 is a deadline for not being dead."

The European Community (EC) did away with most internal tariffs in 1968, but all the remaining nontariff trade barriers are scheduled to be removed by 1992. Under this plan for a single internal market, all obstacles to the free movement of people, goods, services, and money will be abolished.

Workers from any 1 of the 12 countries will be able to take jobs in any of the countries, and passports won't be needed. Diplomas and professional licenses from any 1 of the 12 countries will be recognized in all. A Belgian lawyer will be able to argue a case in British courts; a French doctor will be allowed to treat patients in West Germany.

Consumer products and manufactured goods will be sold freely throughout the EC as long as they meet the standards set by the country where they were made. Trucks crossing country borders will no longer be inspected. The widely differing rates of sales taxes and value added taxes (VATs) will be done away with. Dutch insurance companies will be able to sell life insurance in Great Britain; a French investor will be able to buy stocks on the Italian stock exchange through her Swiss broker.

Foreign exchange controls will be dismantled, bankruptcy and property laws will be standardized, banks will be able to do transactions in each other's currencies, and there eventually will be a single currency in Europe. A West German couple retiring after 1992 will be able to enjoy their new leisure time on their own property in the sunny south of Spain.

For the U.S. businesswoman, the opportunities will be unlimited. A U.S. exporter won't have to develop separate packaging or have a product conform to 12 different country standards. Even greater opportunities exist for U.S. companies that are already positioned in Europe or are planning to set up shop immediately. U.S. companies that want to take advantage of the increased demand in Europe for goods and services such as advertising and marketing, publishing, media, law, and consumer goods only need to get a foothold in one country of the EC to have access to the entire market.

"Europhoria" has struck on both sides of the Atlantic. Many Americans are predicting increased economic growth in Europe after 1992. Europe is already beginning to experience a wave of U.S.-style mergers and acquisitions, shaking up centuries-old corporate cultures.

This excitement is even spreading outside the boundaries of the 12 members of the European Community. Turkey has already applied to join, and Austria and Norway are expected to do so. Some people think Sweden, Switzerland, and Finland may also find the lure of a unified Europe hard to resist.

"The progress of the EC is one of the promising world trends," said Hans-Dietrich Genscher, West Germany's foreign minister. "By creating a community of 12 European democracies, we won a victory over national egoism, power-political thinking and prejudice. It is the greatest and finest victory in the history of Europe. It had not cost one single human life, yet it is winning us the future."

Laws can be changed quickly; centuries-old cultures change much more slowly, if at all. It certainly makes your marketing job easier if your Crispy Flakes breakfast cereal no longer has to meet 12 different sets of nutritional guidelines. But no law will make people in Spain like the same taste in their food as the Swiss. The businesswoman who knows her job will take advantage of European unification, but won't forget all that she has learned about the different cultures and traditions of Europe.

Northern Europe

The Scandinavian countries of Denmark, Norway, Sweden, and Finland are small, modern, and fairly easy for the American business executive to deal in. You can probably call your client by his or her first name after the first few meetings. People are for the most part well-educated, fairly liberal, and friendly.

Your presentations will be heard and given sincere consideration. Be certain of all your facts and quotes. Most Scandinavians speak English very well and enjoy using it. Be punctual for your appointments and avoid becoming involved in discussions of U.S. politics.

There are many people in the United States who have the misguided perception that Scandinavian society is totally liberated and pro-feminist. This is mostly myth; Scandinavian culture is quite traditional, especially in regard to female careerism.

Among these countries, you will find the people in Denmark the most friendly and the most comfortable doing business with women. The Swedes are somewhat more formal and reserved; the Norwegians are also fairly formal, and are more provincial. You will find a few female executives everywhere, but probably more in Finland than in the other Scandinavian countries.

Elsewhere in Europe, you will find that the business culture in the Netherlands (Holland) is somewhat similar to that in Scandinavia. This is also true, to a lesser degree, in Belgium. Punctuality, a certain degree of formality tempered with warmth, and a desire for privacy characterize these countries.

The countries of Germany, Austria, and Switzerland are highly formal in business matters. Using first names is almost unheard of, even among colleagues who have worked together for years. There is more informality among the younger people, but you should always use the titles Mr., Ms., or Doctor to be safe. Punctuality is extremely important in these countries, as is observance of formal social etiquette.

Always begin your meeting with some nonbusiness conversation. Discussing some aspect of the country that you enjoy is a good way to open. Let your client set the pace of the negotiations. Younger Swiss, Austrians, and Germans are somewhat more open and informal, but it's best for you to be conservative in your approach. Moving rapidly into business discussions can set up a somewhat defensive reaction, particularly if you're dealing with the older generation. Your knowledge of your product and of contracts will earn the respect of your client. Once you win your client's confidence, it will be yours forever.

In contrast to the Japanese, many Northern Europeans, particularly Germans, have a low tolerance for ambiguity. Be sure to spell out everything in careful detail. A German contract specifies details that contracts in the United States might leave to standard trade practice.

French businessmen are also somewhat formal and conservative, although not nearly as much as they were 20 years ago. Except for younger or international executives, they do not usually use first names. Using *madame* and *monsieur* without the first name is your best bet. The French often react negatively to new ideas at first, but can be won over after considerable discussion. Rational arguments supported with facts and figures are the most successful tactics. Allow your client sufficient time to examine, question, and talk about all aspects of the deal. Your presentation should be understated and unpressured for the best results.

Southern Europe

Italy is a study in contrasts. Negotiating in Rome, or anywhere to the south, is vastly different from doing business in the northern cities of Milan or Turin. Northern Italy is more like Switzerland in concepts of time and personal space, while Southern Italy is more languid, informal, and macho.

When beginning your meeting it is not necessary to spend much time making conversation. It is perfectly all right to shake hands and begin discussing business after a brief preliminary chat. Your client will expect you to be very well briefed on your products or services, their applications, and what they are being used for in other countries. Most Italian executives will be quite courteous to you and will try to avoid giving a definite "no" answer even if they are not interested in your offer.

Italians are fairly formal in their business dealings, and first names are not generally used. A common honorific is *dottore*, and most executives will respond positively even if they are not Ph.D.s.

When dealing with the Milanese, you will find a stronger business orientation and a more positive attitude toward female executives. Romans and Neapolitans often take U.S. businesswomen less seriously. Of course, you may inquire from what part of Italy your client comes, using a polite approach.

Business should not be discussed at dinner or at an informal gathering. Italians are very family-oriented, and inquiries about family are appreciated. Discussions about sports, particularly soccer, and international affairs are popular.

Doing business in Spain still feels like negotiating in an advanced Latin American nation. While executives in Madrid and Barcelona may have had some contact with businesswomen, they may not be as used to dealing with them as their counterparts in Northern Italy. It is only 15 years or so since the repressive Franco era officially ended with the dictator's death, but there has been tremendous change in that short amount of time. In 1975, it was just barely acceptable, and certainly unusual, for a U.S. businesswoman to take herself to lunch alone at a fashionable executive's restaurant. Now it is more commonplace to see business-suited women in formerly male preserves in Madrid and Barcelona.

When you begin your meeting, always shake hands effusively and pass your card around to everyone. In the past few years, formality has given over to first names after initial introductions. Business in Spain is often conducted over drinks and sometimes over dinner. Always return the invitation if you are asked to dinner. Spaniards are friendly and warm people and, like Italians, are very involved with their families. Another favorite subject is bullfighting. Spaniards take this sport very seriously; even if it is offensive to you, do not comment on it negatively. A much better topic of conversation is the rapid economic growth of the country over the last few years.

Since Spain is still somewhat traditional with regard to attitudes toward Spanish women, it is wise not to discuss the incidence of professional careers among Spanish women with your client. However, Spanish attitudes have begun to change, and recent legislation has given Spanish women far more equal opportunity than they had in the past.

It is easier for a woman to do business in Portugal than in Spain. The culture is less formal and somewhat less male-dominated. Women in Portugal hold more management positions than women in Spain or Great Britain.

When doing business in Greece, you should observe the same guidelines as in Spain or Southern Italy. Although Greek society has traditionally been male-dominated, opportunities for women in business and the professions have been increasing.

Great Britain and Ireland

Don't be misled into thinking that because people in the United States, the United Kingdom, and Ireland all speak English there will be easy understanding and similarities in the manner of doing business. Winston Churchill's comment about "two countries separated by a common language" is nowhere more applicable than in business.

Not only can language be misunderstood, but gestures often have different meanings in the United Kingdom than they do in the United States. Because the English and American languages and social customs are often similar, your caution may be reduced. But the simple hand gesture that in the United States is used on the floor of the commodities exchange to mean buy or sell has an obscene connotation in urban London.

The differences, of course, go much deeper than the obvious ones of language and gesture. The British way of thinking is often radically different from that in the United States. As a result of centuries of doing things in a traditional way, the British have a slight resistance to rapid change, and do not move with the same urgency that Americans do. Not even Londoners share the sense of competitiveness that characterizes business in all large (and many smaller) cities of the United States.

The British prefer to keep their private lives out of the business arena. They will not conduct business 24 hours a day as is often the case in the United States, and their entire pace of business is slower and less frenetic.

When negotiating with your British counterparts, whether in England, Scotland, Wales, or Ireland, be certain to say "British" and never "English." Even when you are in England, many of your clients may be Irish, Scots, or Welsh, and you can avoid uncomfortable political errors if you speak only of "the British."

British business appointments are very punctual, but not always formal. The younger generation of business executives is far more informal than the older one, but exceptions abound. Here, as in almost every country in the world, don't rush. You will probably be offered tea, which you can accept or decline without insulting your client. The British are very fond of Americans for the most part, and often enjoy discussing the United States vis-à-vis the United Kingdom.

The British sense of humor is extremly different from that in the United States. It is often bawdy, and always dry. Most jokes attempted by the British often fail to elicit responses from Americans, and vice versa. Avoid humor unless you have a strong sense of British wit.

Your presentation will always be given a thorough hearing. Be careful to use only standard English, avoiding trendy phrases and words. Your British clients may misunderstand the latest New York or Los Angeles expressions.

There are regrettably few women in management in the United Kingdom, although there are a fair number of women in the professions. There is, however, little resistance to dealing with a woman executive from the United States, in part because England has a woman prime minister and the British are aware of the number of business and professional women in the United States. Combined with respect for U.S. business acumen, this business climate makes negotiating with the British a rewarding experience.

Eastern Europe

Perestroika and *glasnost* are not just new words for a crossword puzzle. They symbolize real change in the Soviet Union and through much of the Eastern bloc. The youthful Soviet leader Mikhail Gorbachev and his attractive, articulate wife Raisa are not only modern in appearance, but are opening up the political and economic structure of the USSR.

Opportunities for foreign business and direct investment are increasing rapidly. The Soviets are eager for Western consumer goods (and, to a lesser extent, industrial goods and financial services) and, to an unprecedented extent, have been allowing U.S. and Western European corporations access to their vast and hitherto untapped markets. The Russians still prefer foreign investment to take the form of joint ventures, but recently have begun allowing foreign firms to control a majority share.

Doing business in the Soviet Union and other Eastern bloc states is still difficult because of entrenched bureaucracies, antiquated regulations, and, especially, the lack of a hard, freely transferable currency. But a determined negotiator can cut through these problems. Perhaps the most effective solution to the lack of hard currency is barter, as illustrated by Pepsi Cola's deal to swap Pepsi concentrate for Russian vodka.

Negotiating in Eastern Europe requires hours of getting to know your client on a personal level, almost as in Japan or Latin America. It is customary to shake hands at the beginning of a meeting, and again when leaving. You should address your client only by his or her formal title, unless you are specifically requested to do otherwise. Be punctual for all meetings, which should always be arranged in advance and reconfirmed two to three days beforehand.

Women are prominent in the professions in Russia and throughout Eastern Europe, but somewhat less so in government and business. Nonetheless, most men with whom you come in contact will be very comfortable dealing with a woman. Once you have developed a personal relationship with your client, you can get down to business. At that point you must have a real command of the hard facts and technical details of your product or proposal; a generalized sales pitch will carry no weight.

The new spirit of openness in the Soviet Union is also spreading to other Eastern bloc countries. Poland's elections in 1989 brought opposition party candidates into government for the first time in Eastern Europe since World War II. Poland, Czechoslovakia, and Hungary are all eager for foreign investment and for Western goods and services, and are compromising some of their rigid policies in order to get them.

Although there are still a multitude of problems facing an American businesswoman in Eastern Europe, there are also many opportunities—and certainly vastly more than there were even five years ago!

7

Doing Business in the World Marketplace: Latin America

Latin America is the name most commonly used to signify Mexico, the Spanish-speaking Caribbean, and Central and South America. Although generally lumped together, these regions are vastly different. While nearly all the countries in Latin America speak Spanish except for Brazil, the people, their culture, and their sensibility diverge widely. The Dominican Republic is as different from Argentina as Greece is from Sweden.

There are over four hundred million people in Latin America, half of whom are under 20 years old. Even though the debt situations of Mexico, Brazil, and Argentina now seem overwhelming, these countries are very fertile future markets for U.S. business. In the last few years, democracy in varying degrees has returned to almost all the countries of South America.

As in the Far East and Southeast Asia, some general observations hold true for most Latin Americans. Most countries have small elite groups that control a good portion of the country's wealth. These are the landowners and big-business owners. There is an emerging middle class, particularly in the newly industrialized countries such as Brazil and Mexico. The largest group is the poor, who are the workers, the poor farmers, and the urban underemployed.

While the overwhelming majority (about 98 percent) of Latin Americans are nominally Catholic, the degree of actual religious observance varies from place to place. Many countries have strongly anticlerical attitudes. Other countries, especially Brazil, combine Catholicism with African-based spirit religions. There is a fairly strong belief in fatalism, the idea that life follows a preordained course in which human fate is determined by the will of God. For the U.S. business executive with a "where there is a will, there is a way" attitude, fatalism can severely disrupt any planning and scheduling and cause tremendous frustration.

The concepts of personalism and dignity strongly affect the workings of Latin American organizations. Personalism, or the recognition of each person as an individual, prevents many Latins from blending in to the anonymous conformity required for smooth organizational functioning. Dignity often prevents Latins from doing whatever is necessary to get the job done if it involves dirtying their hands. Latin America is still very stratified socially, and one is either born "high" or "low." While all this is beginning to change, there is still the combination of fatalism and place (the level at which you are born) that prevents many people in Latin America from striving to get ahead and move up the corporate, educational, or professional ladder.

Decision making in Latin America is affected by this class system as well. The person in authority has the power to make decisions without consulting others. Any questioning of such authority would imply lack of confidence in that person's judgment. A worker or lower authority will not question the decision of the person in charge.

The concept of machismo is not limited to Latin America, but certainly is at its most extreme there. Latin males respond to aggression, heroism, and charisma much more than to logic, persuasion, and consensus. Machismo is often most pervasive at the lower levels of the social scale, where prowess is a substitute for real power. In business negotiations you will be dealing mostly with upper-level, educated, fairly powerful men who are less likely to display overt macho tendencies.

The negotiating situation in Latin America provides women with the opportunity of using another pull style known as attracting. In attracting, you produce desired behavior by providing a positive vision of the future and exploring the common ground. For example, you present the vision of what could be "if only Tadpole Tractors were used" in the construction of new homes for workers. The implication is that your product will lead to comfort, prosperity, jobs, and an improved standard of living.

When you begin meeting with a Latin American, you and your client will spend a good deal of time getting to know each other. As in the Far East and the Arab world, serious business is never conducted until and unless a relationship of trust is established. Greet your client effusively, comment on his healthful appearance, ask after his family, and always mention the rapid development of his country's economy. Make sure you know the names of some local heroes and patriots, sports stars, artists, musicians, or writers. Get to know your client. Show genuine interest, respect, and, above all, have patience.

In Latin America, formalities reign. Always address clients as *senor* (*senhor* in Brazil), *senora* (*senhora*), or *senorita* (*senhorita*); or as Mister, Mrs., and Miss; plus their surname. Use of a first name is insulting unless you have been asked to use it.

Don't discuss politics unless you are asked, but make sure you know about the particular country's political leaders and situation before you begin your meetings.

Do not be surprised if your meetings do not begin on time. In Latin America, time is not perceived in the same way as in the United States. You should arrive for an appointment at the agreed-upon time, but be patient if you have to wait. Your client's lateness or keeping you waiting is not a sign of rudeness or disrespect to you. It is often simply another manifestation of the system of kinship ties, under which a manager or employer's first obligation is to family and friends. A request from or discussion with a friend or family member will always take precedence over the business at hand.

If coffee is offered at the beginning of your negotiations, always accept it. You do not have to drink more than a bit, but to refuse the offer is insulting, especially in those countries where coffee was the main cash crop at one time or other. (Besides, you may find, as I did, that you like the coffee in Latin America better than anywhere else in the world.) If your meeting begins with everyone standing around for a few minutes conversing informally, be very conscious not to step back when a Latin American moves closer to you than you'd like. Their idea of personal space is different from that in the United States. Conversational distance is usually comfortable to us at anywhere from 2 to 3 feet, but for Latin Americans this distance is no further than 12 to 18 inches. Your client is not trying to make sexual advances when he steps closer, and you must avoid the impulse to move away.

There is a widespread belief in all parts of Latin America that people from the United States are cold. Much of this stems from our concept of personal space, and from the way the typical U.S. nuclear family has diminished over the past 25 years. Latins perceive us as lacking in friendship and kinship ties, values that are vital to the Latin personality.

Some of this belief has also come from the insensitivity of U.S. businessmen's dealings with Latin America. The jovial, backslapping, wheeling-and-dealing businessman of the past didn't try to pursue a long-term relationship, but rather took the money and ran, leaving bad feelings behind. In many Latin American countries, most notably Mexico, there is a lingering distrust of U.S. businessmen. Mexican businessmen sometimes attempt to get even by cancelling meetings, making frustrating overtures, dragging out negotiations, and generally exhausting their U.S. counterparts. The Mexicans will then attempt to take advantage of that exhaustion when the businessman loses patience and gives more away in a negotiation than he should.

Don't try to rush negotiations, and don't give up if meetings are cancelled. Continue pursuing your client. After you meet a few times, if all your attempts to begin serious negotiations are thwarted, you may be tempted to give up. Don't! Let a few days pass and begin again. You are only being tested for your sincerity. If you give up easily you won't be regarded as serious. Swallow your anger, forget your pride, and you will prove your sincerity to your client. Once this obstacle has been overcome, your negotiations will be easier. It takes a long time to be trusted and regarded as a friend in Latin America, but once it happens, it is for the long term and can be a vital business advantage.

The businesswoman who succeeds in negotiating will have learned that Latin America is not one country. Although there are exceptions, and some countries fall into more than one category, the 18 nations of Spanish- and Portugese-speaking Latin America in which you are most likely to do business fall into five general groupings. Each of these five markets is different from the others; they have little in common except for language.

Caribbean Latin America

Caribbean Latin America includes Puerto Rico, the Dominican Republic, Panama, Honduras, Caracas and coastal Venezuela, the coastal cities of Colombia such as Barranquilla and Cali, and the

Spanish-speaking population of Miami and Tampa, Florida. This group is characterized by a tropical climate, a fairly large black or creole poor population (except in Florida), and a small upper class that controls most of industry and politics. People are warm, open, and friendly, and often admire the United States. Most industry is labor-intensive and low-tech.

While you will encounter a good deal of machismo in these areas, as in many less-developed countries, it will not seriously hinder your progress. Your negotiations are apt to be slow, interrupted, repetitive, and occasionally neglected. Adapt a non-presuming but formal stance, retain your sense of humor, and have patience.

Mexico

Mexico is in a category by itself because of its strategic importance to U.S. business and the difficulty of negotiating there. Mexicans have never forgotten the U.S. annexation of the Southwest. This fact, combined with extreme nationalism, fatalism, the current debt and inflation situation, and, paradoxically, a pervasive belief in the superiority of U.S. goods, makes for a love-hate relationship between the Mexican people and U.S. visitors. Mexicans are very proud of the progress they have made independent of U.S. influence. It is a good idea to learn about Mexico's economic accomplishments and to praise them effusively.

Although it is probably not a good idea for you to discuss Mexican politics, you should know a little about current events in our southern neighbor. In 1988, Carlos Salinas de Gortari took office after the closest presidential election in Mexican history. The once-omnipotent PRI (Institutional Revolutionary Party) lost the election for the state governorship to conservatives in Baja California Norte in 1989, suggesting that Mexico may be on the verge of a genuine multiparty system.

Salinas has begun a crackdown on widespread corruption and has forced Mexican investors to repatriate about one billion dollars in capital. He has also opened Mexico's stock exchange to foreign investment, invited private investors to take over state-owned industries, and cut red tape for major multinational corporations to increase spending on new projects as well as plants and equipment. If all goes as planned, this will provide renewed opportunities for U.S. corporations to step up their dealings with Mexico. There has even been some discussion of Mexico eventually signing a free trade pact like that between the United States and Canada, although that is not likely in the immediate future. But for now, there's a good deal of business developing between the United States and Mexico that you and your company should be looking into.

Do not expect your appointments in Mexico to begin on time. Even Mexican businessmen joke about specifying *hora Americana* (U.S. time), as distinguished from Mexican time, when they want to indicate punctuality. Remember that Mexicans are North Americans, so be sensitive when discussing geographic regions. Never call people from the United States "Americans."

Mexico's proximity to the United States hasn't benefitted Mexican women much yet in the professional sphere. It will take some work for your Mexican client to get used to you and accept you. Be cordial but firm. Mexico is probably as difficult a place for U.S. businessmen to negotiate in as for women because of the fear and hostility created by images of "big brother from the North" returning to pillage.

It is very helpful to know at least a few words of Spanish, and if at all possible a few of the Mexican idioms. While many Mexicans speak English very well, you may encounter some executives who staunchly refuse to use it in the negotiating process. Be certain to find out in advance if you may speak English at your meetings. It may be useful to have an interpreter along in any case. In the course of contract negotations in Mexico, remember that Mexicans treat the contract as a work of art and an expression of the ideal. A contract expresses a goal to be strived for, not a binding obligation expected to apply consistently in the real world.

You will probably encounter more macho attitudes in Mexico than in any other part of Latin America except for the Caribbean. While this may be off-putting, remember that Mexico is a huge and growing market of over 75 million people right on the southern border of the United States. The proximity, size, and demand of the Mexican market make it worth your while in spite of all the cancelled, forgotten, or ignored meetings and other frustrations and delays.

Brazil

Brazil, the third category, is somewhat different from the rest of Latin America as it is the only Portugese-speaking country on the continent. Brazilians are sometimes called *Luso-Americans* (derived from Lusitinia, the ancient name for Portugal). Brazil is a huge country with over 130 million people. The first civilian presidential election in 21 years was held in 1985, and put a democratic government in office. Inflation is high, and Brazil owes nearly one hundred billion dollars in external debt. Nevertheless, Brazil is an excellent place in which to do business for the long term. One window of opportunity that was opened in 1989 was Brazil's removal of the restriction on importing computer technology. Quietly and informally, the government has been allowing everything from computerized electronic fuel injection components to software to be brought in.

Half the population of Brazil is under 20 years old, and there is tremendous pent-up demand. U.S. goods are highly valued and sought-after. The Brazilians admire the United States and its economic strength. There is a positive attitude on the part of the Brazilians toward doing business with us.

It is important to remember when exchanging business cards that in Brazil, Paulo Lopes Almeida is called Senhor Almeida. Brazil differs from Spanish-speaking Latin America in this regard; in Mexico (and other Spanish-speaking countries), José Garcia Rodriguez is called Senor Garcia, never Senor Rodriguez.

Brazilians have a great zest for life, and nowhere is this more evident than in Rio de Janeiro. Your meetings in Rio will be relatively informal in nature with an unhurried pace. The south, especially São Paulo, is far more European and business-like in style.

When you sit down at the negotiating table you will be offered coffee. Never refuse it, as coffee provided the cash to build the great cities of Brazil. You don't have to drink it all; a sip will do as long as it is followed by a comment on how delicious it is. Milk will not be served along with it, but you will be given sugar and a glass of cold water. The drink is powerful, but this is what coffee is all about!

Knowing a handful of words of Portugese earns you respect automatically, because any number of U.S. businessmen before you have made the inexcusable error of using Spanish at their meetings. Many Brazilians in executive positions speak English well, but you should always be sure to ask in advance if you may speak English as in a few cases you may need an interpreter. Whatever you do, don't speak Spanish. Brazilians understand Spanish, but are proud of being different from their Spanish-speaking neighbors and regard the use of Spanish as insulting. Begin your discussions with comments on the rapid growth of the country's cities, the beauty of its beaches, and similar topics.

There is a great internal competition between the cities of Rio and São Paulo (São is pronounced something like the English word "sound" without the "d"). Rio is said to be the heart of Brazil and São Paulo the pocketbook. Differences between Cariocas (those who live in Rio) and Paulistas (residents of São Paulo) are much like those between Los Angelinos and New Yorkers. A popular Brazilian newspaper cartoon shows a bikinied man and woman on a beach in Rio watching a man in a suit carrying a briefcase and hurrying across the beach. The caption says, "That's our new neighbor who recently moved here from São Paulo."

São Paulo, in the south of Brazil, is a great industrial center, looking more like Chicago than anywhere else. Business there is formal, intense, and punctual. The pace is fast and relatively straightforward. As opposed to tropical Rio, São Paulo has a more temperate climate, and its inhabitants have a tremendous zest for doing business. While you still have to observe rituals such as coffee drinking and introductory discussions, you will probably be able to conclude negotiations faster here than in Rio or other Brazilian cities such as Brasilia (the capital) or Belo Horizonte.

Brazil's ethnic makeup is fascinating. The population is composed of largely European stock in the southern states of São Paulo and Rio Grande do Sul, blacks in the Northeast, and Indians in the still partly unexplored northwest. You will encounter every skin color and ethnic combination.

You will find much less machismo in Brazil than in Mexico. Women are often in the professions such as medicine, education, and journalism, and occasionally are small-business owners. While few Brazilian women are in managerial or executive capacities, as an American woman you will find little resistance to doing business in Brazil.

European Latin America

European Latin America includes Argentina, Costa Rica, Chile, Colombia, Uruguay, the city of Lima in Peru, and the aforementioned southern part of Brazil. Aside from Argentina, you will find negotiating in these countries and cities the most familiar and the most like Western Europe of all Latin America.

Argentina and Uruguay in particular identify very strongly with European traditions and ways of life. While both countries have had a long history of right-wing leaders, they now have democratically elected presidents who seem to be improving the overall economy. At the turn of the century, Argentina was the economic equal of

Canada, but it has steadily declined. Argentina, with a long history of fascism, political instability, foreign debt, and inflation, is a difficult country in which to work.

In 1989 Argentina elected Peronist Carlos Menem as president. He went on to appoint free-market advocates to his new government, departing greatly from Peronist tradition. Although it's too soon to know if this new government can cure Argentina's hyperinflation and general economic crisis, Menem has certainly taken steps in the right direction.

Argentines are very proud, sometimes to the point of arrogance; as reported in the *New York Times* on April 25, 1982, they consider "Brazilians monkeys and Americans [U.S.] uncultured." They are educated and sophisticated, and believe that Buenos Aires (the capital of Argentina) is a spiritual outpost of Paris. In many ways they're right. Portenos (residents of Buenos Aires) are chauvinistic, secretive, and difficult to warm up to. The capital is lovely, and if you squint, the boulevards do seem to resemble those of Paris. The pinstriped men, the activity of the *bolsa* (stock exchange), and the general demeanor do in fact recall Paris. You can break down Argentines' resistance to you personally, and in doing business, by acknowledging this resemblance and commenting favorably on their sophistication, charm, and European graciousness.

In Bogota, Colombia (although not too much trade is occurring there today other than drug traffic); in Lima, Peru; and in Chile and Costa Rica, you will be able to conduct your negotiations in a manner similar to that in most of Western Europe. These people are gracious, formal, and receptive to U.S. executives. Chile is the only country in Latin America still under a powerful dictatorship, but free elections have been promised for 1990. Chile's economy declined sharply in the early years of the dictatorship, but has rebounded in the 1980s. Chilean women are educated and, at least before the repressive dictatorship of the 1970s and 1980s, were quite liberated and outspoken.

Chile, a free-market economy with the best performance in Latin America, has become the envy of many countries in the region. It is prospering economically with booming exports of fruit, vegetables, fish, and metals. Investment is strong, and growth has averaged 5 percent a year in the period 1985–1989.

Your negotiations in European Latin America will be fairly punctual, formal, and reserved. Coffee will be served and you should always accept it. Observe the general guidelines for doing business in Europe.

Indian Latin America

Indian Latin America includes Bolivia, Paraguay, and Ecuador in South America, and Guatemala and El Salvador in Central America.

While Spanish is spoken in the large cities, the rural areas speak Indian dialects almost exclusively. Even in the cities, negotiations will be slow and drawn-out. People are generally courteous, friendly, and steeped in Indian tradition. As a result you must be patient in negotiating and continually reiterate the important details. It will take quite some time to complete your dealings, but perseverance will pay off.

8

Doing Business in the World Marketplace: Africa and the Middle East

The Middle East

The Middle East is by far the most difficult area for the U.S. businesswoman. Indeed, there are a few places, like Saudi Arabia, that make it extremely difficult for women even to obtain business visas. Nevertheless, there are a number of countries, despite the increasing Arabization of the Middle East, where women can work quite comfortably.

The 20 or so nations of the Arab world contain more than two hundred million people. Western business executives are traveling to the Middle East in increasing numbers. The wealth of this region and its emergence as the world's major oil producer has made it enormously important to the United States and to every country dependent on imported oil.

As a result of the U.S. support of Israel, there is long-standing antagonism toward us in the Arab world. There is an effort in some Arab countries to boycott private companies doing business in Israel. Before any attempt to do business in the Arab world is undertaken, be sure to check the minutest regulations of the country far in advance of any planned visits.

As in Asian cultures, the concept of face is extremely important in the Arab world. Arabs are very sensitive to small slights and embarrassments. Avoid any situations that make your client look bad. This sensitivity is related to religion, rank, nationality, and class. You should carefully research the country in which you will do business to learn the many nationalities and minorities both within the country and without, and their current alliances and hostilities. Intra-Arab fighting has been virulent in the past few years, with more than a few countries continually at war with each other.

Although the Arab world is varied, there are some generalizations that hold for the entire area. The most important factor to consider is the religion, Islam, which dominates life in the Middle East. Many of the restrictions on women derive from Islam's emphasis on traditional values and behavior. Moslems believe that open social relations between the sexes result in the breakdown of family life.

The concept of the family network, quite unknown in the West, can almost be compared to our social welfare system. Nepotism here (as in Latin America) is not a negative concept; it is expected and congratulated. These kinship ties operate at all levels of society and business.

In the Arab world there is a rigid concept of what work is dignified and allowed. Saudis and some other Arabs will not do any manual labor. They will hire Sudanese or Yemenis to do the dirty work. People are expected to know their place and few try to change their lot. This corresponds roughly to the Latin American sense of place and fatalism, and the belief in God's will.

As in Asian culture, there is great respect for age. Advanced years mean wisdom and command respect. Age takes precedence even over rank. Also, the outright "no" is never given, either in business or in social situations. You should avoid the absolute negative in your negotiations. Do not confuse a genuine "maybe" with the "maybe" that really means the unspeakable "no." If you have been avoided or turned aside a number of times, this means that the "maybe" is really "no."

Concepts of time and space in the Middle East are similar to those in Latin America, and "tomorrow" isn't always meant literally. Don't be put off by broken appointments. Continue making new appointments and don't show your irritation.

People often sit or stand very close to each other in Arab business negotiations. Part of this has to do with the practice of holding at least three meetings concurrently. In order to capture each other's attention, Arabs literally must speak into each other's ears. You probably will not have the problem of uncomfortable closeness, however. A woman doing business here is so unusual, given the negative Arab attitude toward women, that they will prrobably stand a good distance away, if they will do business with you at all.

Most Arabs will do business with a woman, but only if they know who she is and trust her. While a Western woman will never be fully accepted in the Arab social world, there is no reason why she can't develop a relationship of trust with her client. There is no doubt that it will take longer to establish this relationship than perhaps in any other region, but it can be done using patience, respect for Moslem tradition, and a genuine desire to become friends. If your client wants your product or service, and you are professional, he will accept you.

Among the Arab countries, Egypt is a relatively comfortable place for women to do business. Cairo and Alexandria are sophisticated and cosmopolitan cities. Egyptians are friendly and liberal by Arab standards. There is no segregation of the sexes, and it is legal to drink alcohol in Egypt. Most of your clients will speak English quite well. The capital, Cairo, is a large and crowded city of almost ten million people.

You will be at a distinct advantage if you invite your client and his wife to a European-style restaurant along with a few of his associates and their wives. Women are very much a part of social and business life in Egypt. In your negotiations, take the time to know your client. While business will not progress as quickly as in Western European countries or Israel, Egyptians are quite Westernized and are comfortable dealing with business executives from the United States and Europe.

Jordan is also a somewhat liberal Arab country, with women welcomed in public life. Always accept coffee offered by your client at meetings, as it is the custom. There will probably be some surprise at your being a woman, but you will not have any major problems doing business.

You can easily obtain a visa for both Egypt and Jordan. All business travelers need a supporting letter from their company explaining the nature of business and confirming their financial solvency. All Arab countries (except Egypt, which has had a peace treaty with Israel since 1982) make it difficult or impossible for a businessperson to enter the country if their passport shows evidence of a visit to Israel.

Aside from Egypt and Jordan, you should observe strict Moslem protocols in doing business in the Middle East, both in the more liberal Arab countries (Bahrain, Kuwait, and the United Arab Emirates) as well as in the more traditional ones. In Saudi Arabia or other very traditional countries you will probably not be allowed to meet your client in his office, and your meeting may take place in a private home. Moreover, you will have to be sponsored, probably by an embassy, a Saudi family, a corporation, or even your husband or father!

In any case, be punctual even if you have to wait. As soon as you enter the client's office (or the client meets you at his home) present your two-sided business card, Arabic side up. Make small talk and avoid discussion of any other countries in the region. Arab disunity and intra-Arab hostility are widespread. Always accept and drink (with your right hand only) the hot tea or coffee offered. It is a good idea to drink more than one cup, if possible. If you don't want any more, shake the empty cup when returning it. This signifies your refusal.

After pleasantries have been exchanged and your client indicates that business may begin, start your presentation. Prepare it in small segments as there will often be interruptions. People may wander in and out of your meeting unannounced. Try not to lose your concentration. This is not rudeness, but just a different way of doing business. Don't become exasperated or feel insulted. Serial meetings are not the rule in the Arab world; rather, several meetings may take place virtually simultaneously.

Your meeting may also be interrupted at one of the five daily Moslem prayer times which occur at dawn, noon, mid-afternoon, early evening, and late evening. The faithful will stop discussions and kneel to pray. Be careful not to walk on a prayer mat, don't stare, and never interrupt. These prayers last only a few minutes at most. You should simply sit quietly and wait.

During your meeting, be careful not to hand your client any papers with your left hand. If you are left-handed, take extra caution. The left hand is considered unclean, and using it is an extreme insult.

Take care to avoid any business trips to the region during the month of Ramadan, when Moslems are forbidden to eat, smoke, or drink from dawn to dusk! The month of Ramadan does not correspond to any particular month of the Western calendar, so be careful to check before your trip.

After you have made your presentation and drunk your final cup of coffee, it is time to take the initiative in leaving. If your client wants you to remain or continue, he will urge you to do so; if not, this indicates that he has heard as much of your proposal as he intends to hear.

Arab businessmen put religion and family before business. Deadlines do not have the same impact on Arabs that they do on Westerners. Time is not considered controllable by human beings, and God's will cannot be changed. All this makes for a way of conducting business that seems very unusual to a U.S. executive. Since almost everything is deemed more important than negotiating, meetings may be put off or ended abruptly.

Try to avoid direct eye contact with Arabs, especially in Saudi Arabia. Most people in the United States believe that eye contact is a prerequisite for an honest relationship, but many Arabs are adept at reading the response of your pupils, which dilate when you are really interested in something and contract when you feel dislike.

While most Arabs speak English, it is a good idea to know a few words of Arabic. Be certain to find out in advance if you'll need an interpreter. Rank is important when dealing with Arabs, particularly the Saudis. They want to deal with someone who has decision-making authority. If they think you are not of sufficiently high rank they may take it as an insult, since they will interpret this to mean that your company does not consider the Saudi or the project important enough to send a person of rank. This can easily become a reason for them to back out of a project or refuse to deal with you.

In most cases you will want to know the reasons for changes in attitude or interest in your project. Stay alert to your client's moods and try to turn things around if you feel your client is losing interest. Women have an advantage here as their sensitivity to mood changes is frequently greater than men's.

As in China, Saudis will always let you know that you are competing against other companies. They often will know prices and terms that other companies can offer even though they are dealing only with your company. This is a way for your client to show that he is knowledgeable and not gullible.

Alternate currencies such as training in the United States for your client, his son, or managers; an invitation to the United States for business or vacation; or any personal assistance for your client and his family will make a great difference in the outcome of your negotiations. By offering to help your client's family you will have gotten to the center of his life. This is the real focus of a Saudi's (and most Arabs') life. It will endear you to him, and may possibly be the determining factor in achieving a successful outcome.

One place in the region where you can do business without restrictions placed on women is Israel. While Israeli society is aggressive and male-dominated, women can negotiate in Western style. Despite the recent political instability in the Israeli-occupied West Bank, Israel still has a very strong relationship with the United States and actively seeks to do business with U.S. firms. Israel's fast-growing, innovative technological base makes it an attractive country for investment, countertrade, licensing and franchising arrangements, and all forms of joint ventures.

When you sit down at the negotiating table in Israel, be prepared for aggressive bargaining. Israelis are demanding and the business pace is very fast by Middle Eastern standards. While macho attitudes always prevail, you can, by taking the time to learn a little about Israel's recent history, strike a deal in a fairly short time. Almost all Israelis speak English as it is uniformly taught in the schools. Be firm, polite, and friendly.

India

India is an immense and diverse country of over 750 million people. The large majority (80 percent) of Indians are Hindus, but there are significant numbers of Moslems and Sikhs. There are 14 languages spoken in addition to English. To be on the safe side, when meeting with your Indian client, offer a *namaste* instead of a handshake: Place both hands together as in the position for a prayer, and make a slight bow. If you are sure that your client is very Westernized, offer your hand. It is generally not a good idea to discuss the weather in India as it is almost always hot and somewhat uncomfortable.

Part of the legacy that years of British rule left in India is a multilayered bureaucracy. Your negotiations may have to go through several levels of management before any progress is made. Be patient. This huge democracy has a promising market. Be cautious, however. Everyone in India (or so it seems) wants to do business with the United States. Research your client thoroughly before beginning labyrinthine meetings.

Pakistan

Although it is a predominantly Moslem country, Pakistan's new prime minister is a young woman, Benazier Bhutto. Educated in the West, this daughter of former prime minister Zulfikar Ali Bhutto was elected in 1988. After 11 years of military rule and an "Islamization" campaign that diminished women's rights, Pakistan's one hundred million people now have a leader with promise. Under the previous regime, women were generally encouraged to withdraw from public life. Prime Minister Bhutto's victory and presence have given a much-needed boost to a country whose women had been in danger of being reduced to worthlessness.

Karachi, the largest city, is the primary center of business. English is widely spoken there. When you invite your client for a meal, do not suggest alcohol. In fact, you are not allowed to consume it in public, but in the big hotels it may be obtained (only by non-Moslems).

Many of the customs are similar to those of India. Pakistan came into existence in 1947 after the partition of British India into (primarily Hindu) India and (primarily Moslem) Pakistan, but you should *never* refer to India. There is still great rivalry between the countries, and for many Pakistanis, relations with India are measured in wars. Whatever you do, do not discuss politics, although you may remark on your pleasure in seeing a woman prime minister, as Benazir Bhutto is an extremely popular national heroine.

Africa

As in Latin America, Africa is the term used to describe a continent. But like Latin America, Africa is not a monolithic culture. The six hundred million people who live in Africa speak hundreds of languages, and come from a variety of ethnic and rural backgrounds. Although U.S. investments have generally declined in black Africa over the past few years, there are still many opportunities for conducting business.

Nigeria, the largest country in Africa, is situated on the west coast. Lagos is the capital city of this country of more than 110 million people. Although the official language is English, and upper-class clubs and restaurants are quite British in nature, it is important to remember that 44 percent of the population of Nigeria is Moslem. In fact, many black African nations have a high proportion of Moslems, and the same rules that apply to Moslem Arabic nations should be respected here as well.

Nigeria is a relatively prosperous country whose fortunes ebb and flow with the price of oil, its largest export. While Nigeria, like many of its neighbors, faces problems of political instability, corruption among the bureaucracy, and poverty and illiteracy among the population, there is a fair amount of opportunity to do business in Nigeria, especially in sophisticated Lagos. The educated young Nigerians are upwardly mobile and have a great appreciation of Western values.

Nigeria has a thriving communications industry; you will find sophisticated advertising in newspapers and magazines, and on radio and TV. Most of the media are headquartered in the capital city, Lagos.

When conducting business, gender may be less an issue than race. It is conceivable that a U.S. woman, either black or white, would have an easier time in Nigeria than a white male, since she won't remind Nigerians of their former colonizers!

Just as in most of Asia and Latin America, the way to do business in Africa is through personal contacts and if at all possible with the support, or at very least the friendship, of the highest-ranking national executive. Some Americans have been successful in investing in plants and equipment in the Congo because they courted that country's president. They have little trouble breaking through bureaucratic barriers after showing a picture of themselves with the president at his palace.

Out of the ten million inhabitants of the French-speaking Ivory Coast, over four million depend on their country's leading crop—the world's best cocoa—for their living. Abidjan, the capital, is a thriving commercial city with sophisticated restaurants and hotels.

Next door to the Ivory Coast is English-speaking Ghana, which has prospered over the last five years. This nation of 14 million people has been chosen by the World Bank to be one of the largest recipients of interest-free loans. While the standard of living and per capita income are still quite low compared to the Ivory Cost, there are strong investor commitments for improvement. In all Ghanaian business dealings, the personal approach is essential.

Kenya is one of the most developed countries in Africa. Its industry and government center is in Nairobi. Here, as in Nigeria, the British influence is evident, and the business visitor can feel comfortable speaking English and observing the usual Western customs. Business is often conducted through local agents who stock goods and offer servicing facilities. Keep in mind the fact that overseas buying is usually confined to products not manufactured locally. If you have new products to introduce to Kenya, you'll have to deal with the government's chief purchasing officer in Nairobi.

There are very good restaurants in Kenya as well as Rotary and Lion's clubs in which to entertain your client. You can also apply for temporary memberships at private clubs, where good sports and dining facilities exist. Make all inquiries and applications before you leave for Kenya so you won't waste precious time while you're there.

Zimbabwe, formerly Rhodesia, is a small, clean, almost European-feeling country. Recently Zimbabwe announced a new investment code that represents a departure from the country's previous socialist economic orientation. The finance minister of this nation of nine million people is "dedicated to transforming the social system so that the poorest can be included." Previously, only the U.S. food giant H. J. Heinz had a majority interest in a company here. Investment had been nil because Zimbabwe refused to sign an agreement with the Overseas Private Investment Corporation (OPIC), a U.S. agency that insures American investments against seizure or interference with profits getting to the parent company. Tony O'Reilly, the chairman of Heinz, formed a close relationship with Zimbabwe's president Robert Mugabe, the leader of what is considered one of the most stable countries in the continent. Recently, however, Zimbabwe has liberalized its economic policies, and has adopted a new investment code that should create new opportunities for U.S. business.

Bordering Zimbabwe is South Africa, a country with which the United States once had strong economic ties. However, in reaction to the repressive apartheid policies of South Africa's white minority regime, the United States (along with most European and African nations) is increasingly boycotting South Africa.

9

Doing Business in the World Marketplace: The United States and Canada

Canada

Europe, as we have seen, is beginning the arduous process of consolidating 12 wildly disparate cultures into a single market of 320 million consumers. The United States, however, with 240 million people, shows how culturally and economically diverse a society can remain even after two hundred years of political unity. At the same time, there has been talk, since the ratification in 1988 of the U.S.-Canada Trade Pact, of a "North American, Inc." free trade block, which would add another 26 million English- and French-speaking Canadians to this dynamic market.

The almost-four-thousand mile border between the United States and Canada is the largest unguarded border in the world. Although it's true that Vancouver has more in common with Seattle than it does with Winnipeg, which in turn resembles Minneapolis more than it does Toronto, Canadians—contrary to some people's belief—are not occupants of the 51st state, but have an identity very much their own.

The relationship between the two countries has always been quite close. Currently, over $150 billion a year in trade flows between the United States and Canada. Nonetheless, despite this economic cooperation, Canadians have always struggled to maintain a cultural identity distinct from that of the United States, even though they have not always succeeded. It was this emotional desire for cultural separateness, more than economic issues, that spurred the vigorous (albeit unsuccessful) opposition to the trade pact. This same spirit was revealed in a recent television show when former prime minister Pierre Trudeau told a group of visitors from the United States that "living next door to you is in some ways like sleeping with an elephant. No matter how friendly and even-tempered the beast, one is affected by every twitch and grunt."

Opposition to what is perceived as U.S. "domination" is strongest in the French-speaking province of Quebec. While the United States has always aspired to the ideal of a "melting pot" of assimilated immigrants, Canada has two main, geographically separated ethnic enclaves, the English-speaking and the French-speaking. Tensions have often flared between the two. Recently, a columnist in a leading newspaper in Montreal (a predominantly French-speaking city in the province of Quebec) predicted that "In 50 years, Canada will not exist as we know it. Quebec will no longer be part of the Federation." Other observers, however, are more optimistic both about the future unity of Canada, and about the future of U.S.-Canadian economic cooperation. There are vast opportunities in Canada for Americans, and the United States will continue to becken to Canadian business to cross our borders. Some Canadians object to the proliferation of the McDonald's franchises or U.S.-made television shows, but this is only half the story. While eating Hardees fast food, sipping an alcoholic or soft drink from Seagrams, or sitting in an apartment or office leased by Olympia-York, people in the United States may feel they are patriotic consumers. Actually, these are all Canadian companies that have become assimilated into the U.S. culture.

Toronto, a clean and upwardly mobile city, is Canada's capital of commerce. English-speaking Toronto, with its universities, museums, and restaurants, combines the best of North American culture and industry in an attractive environment. While Toronto might remind you of a cleaner, quieter Chicago, Montreal has a far more European feel to it. Winnipeg, Ottawa, and Vancouver are also cities in which women can comfortably live, work, and successfully conduct business. The city of Quebec, on the other hand, is the center of French nationalist feelings, and any business visitor who doesn't speak French will meet with difficulty.

Negotiating with Canadians is fairly easy, providing you don't use the rapid-fire pace associated with cities such as New York and Chicago. Except for the more rural parts of the province of Quebec, where the traditional family still reigns, Canadians are quite receptive to managerial women. Don't lose sight, however, of the cultural differences that exist in the negotiating process. The Canadian way is to approach new topics subtly and obliquely rather than head-on. Canadians tend to be modest and relatively quiet. Respect these differences and use your courteous style, and you're sure to succeed in any venture with the Canadians.

The free trade agreement and a gradual loosening of local regulations make this an opportune time for Canadian service businesses to open up to U.S. joint ventures, acquisitions, and branch offices. Advertising and law are two areas of opportunity that will experience growth. Similarly, the trade pact and Canada's relaxed restrictions on financial service institutions will lead to increased growth for U.S. banking operations in Canada.

If Canada's big cities don't have quite the number of executive and professional women that the biggest U.S. cities do, Canadian boards of directors are more likely to include women, according to a recent study by Korn/Ferry International. Also, recent affirmative action legislation has ensured more equal opportunities in areas previously resistant to women and minorities.

Ontario, Canada's largest province, recently enacted legislation requiring all employers, public and private, to equalize the pay of jobs traditionally held by women with traditionally male jobs involving comparable "skill, effort, responsibility and working conditions."

The U.S.-Canada Trade Agreement has provided win-win situations for both countries, so opportunities for successful business dealings between the United States and Canada will continue to abound in the future.

The United States

Moving to the south, we come to the vast United States, which some say is the only country where "a poor boy (or girl) can grow up to be president." In fact, the United States is one of the few places on earth where you can change the social status of your birth. The patron saint of the entrepreneur, Uncle Sam, has overseen thousands of people become millionaires. I came from poverty, but I was able to educate myself into prosperity, like many others. These opportunities for advancement have attracted wave after wave of foreign immigration to the United States. Despite the aspirations to be a melting pot, the United States retains a diversity that makes it the most dynamic and exciting market in the world.

Traveling today between Miami, with its almost Caribbean style and climate, and frigid Boston with its blue-blooded Brahmins and its Route 128 techies, can be as much of a culture shock as traveling between Greece and Germany.

And travel we will. In 1988 over 130 million business trips were made in the United States. In less than ten years, approximately 50 percent of the business travelers in the United States will be women. In 1987 alone, American women took 47.2 million business trips. Crisply tailored women have been a common sight in New York, Chicago, and Los Angeles for some time, but in Tulsa or Tuscaloosa a woman attending a major closing might still raise an eyebrow or two. But even this is changing.

Not only are the airlines and large hotel chains getting used to seeing women carrying briefcases and two-suit valet packs, even small motels and coffee shops in regions where business was formerly a male-only preserve are starting to welcome the presence of businesswomen.

Women traveling alone are being made to feel more welcome by rental car companies, airlines, and, especially, hotels. When women began traveling extensively in the late 1970s and early 1980s, hotels went overboard trying to attract women. The result was too much pastel and not enough serious thought given to the needs of a woman executive. Now, instead of patronizing attitudes, most hotels are offering improved security, more suites or rooms with a separate area for entertaining clients (for women who are uncomfortable discussing business with a male colleague in a bedroom), more varied room service, and even special computer-monitored in-room bar service (for women who don't want to fight off lounge lizards). Some major hotel chains have special training programs in which employees learn to treat women traveling alone with appropriate respect. I have been received particularly graciously at Hyatt, Hilton, and Marriott hotels in various locations.

Airlines are also becoming more sensitive to women traveling in business. On a recent coast-to-coast flight on American Airlines, the flight attendant saw me struggling in my seat with my mass of reports, and invited me to move to a less crowded part of the plane where I could spread out my papers.

Once a businesswoman is comfortably ensconced in a hotel, perhaps with her rental car in the well-lighted garage, she is ready to go out and make the sale, negotiate the contract, or visit the client for an introductory meeting. But how well she succeeds may have less to do with her ability than the simple fact of where she is! A recent study by Texas A&M University's College of Business Administration shows that executive and managerial women were more accepted in the West and the Northeast United States than in the South or Midwest. Nationally, a majority of executives polled expressed favorable attitudes toward women in management; but when the figures were broken down by region, almost 65 percent of the Western and 57 percent of the Eastern respondents indicated favorable attitudes, compared with 48 percent of the Southern and 40 percent of the Midwestern respondents.

So, if your territory potentially can include the West or Northeast, or if you are interested in moving to an area where businesswomen are highly regarded and where the women's share of executive/managerial jobs exceeds 35 percent, you might want to explore career opportunities in some of the more favorable areas.

Another consideration worth noting is that if you are interested in getting into international business at some time in the future, working on the West Coast with its strong Pacific orientation is good preparation for working in Asia, and working in the Northeast, with its old-world establishment style and ties to Western Europe, can provide opportunities for work there.

The West has always been the upstart, and in many cases has been the originator of trends that spread rapidly to the Northeast and then are assimilated by the rest of the country. Alfalfa sprout salads and tofuburgers, now standard fare in big cities, could only have started in California.

The state of Washington has an equal rights amendment. State and city contracts guarantee pay equity, and state law guarantees maternity leave. With those inducements, it's little wonder that women have a 43.6 percent share of the managerial and executive jobs in Seattle, the "capital of the Pacific Northwest." Physically appealing, reasonably priced, and populated with genuinely nice people, Seattle heads many lists as one of the best places in the United States for women to work and live. Although the pace is considerably less frantic than in other large cities, business is conducted in a straightforward manner.

Also high on the list of best cities for women is San Francisco, with a whopping 45.6 percent as women's share of managerial and executive jobs. San Francisco, which has been called "an East Coast city on the West Coast," combines the best of both worlds. In addition, state and city contracts guarantee pay equity, and state law guarantees some maternity leave. This is a truly cosmopolitan city which has taken steps to limit its growth. To Northeasterners' minds, San Francisco resembles nothing so much as New York City shrunk to manageable proportions. Other cities worth investigating in the Pacific Northwest region are Olympia, Spokane, and Tacoma in Washington state, and Portland and Eugene in Oregon, all of which have a strong "quality of life" orientation.

Moving south down the West Coast, we come to the great metropolis of Los Angeles, which is quickly outstripping San Francisco as the financial services center of the West Coast. Los Angeles was once considered a cultural wasteland, but it is now opening art galleries, restaurants, and quality museums at an amazing rate. Japanese business is increasingly conducted from Los Angeles. California First Bank, a subsidiary of the Bank of Tokyo and the largest Japanese-owned bank in California, is planning to move its headquarters from San Francisco to Los Angeles. California is scheduled to deregulate banking in 1991, and many banks from the United States and all over the world are expected to begin operations there.

The accent in Los Angeles is obviously on physical appearance, due to year-round warm weather and, of course, Hollywood. But unless you are in the highly competitive entertainment industry, you needn't "take" a meeting, "do" lunch, or feel over the hill at 35! Women's share of executive and managerial jobs here is almost 40 percent and growing, and women serve as mayors of several Los Angeles-area communities.

Houston, Texas, the largest city in the country, has a woman mayor (Kathy Whitemore) and a fairly high women's share of managerial and executive jobs for the Southwest region.

Opportunities for women are plentiful in the "Northeast corridor" (an airline and railroad expression that includes Boston, New York, and Washington, D.C.).

Boston, although famous for its large academic "industry," is more than just a college town. Its culture and arts emphasis, its state ERA, and its gentrified atmosphere (reflected in its high per capita consumption of white wine), make it a comfortable environment for a professional woman. The cost of living is high, but is considered well worth the price by Bostonians. Cambridge, Boston's sister city and the home of Harvard and M.I.T., is reminiscent of Berkeley, California, just as Boston itself is reminiscent of San Francisco and nearby

Route 128 is the East Coast's answer to Silicon Valley. "Pahk yah cah neah Hahvahd Yahd," and close that deal!

The next stop on the Northeast corridor is New York City, the "Big Apple." (The name can now even be found in the dictionary.) New York City has both the best and worst of all worlds. For art, music, restaurants, film, theater, architecture, and literature, all concentrated within a few square miles, there is no equal. Yet sky-high prices, noise, and crime can lessen the charm for some. At night the skyline sparkles, and by day the pace is frantic and competitive, but there are tremendous opportunities for women here. Meetings are often rushed, pressured affairs, but the two-martini business lunch is a thing of the past, and working lunches today are apt to consist of tuna salad and Perrier for everyone! There are hundreds of professional women's organizations, associations, and networks; women from southern Westchester County, southern Connecticut, and New Jersey are all part of this greater New York milieu. Media, advertising, banking, retailing, sales, fashion, and small-business ownership all boast huge numbers of upwardly mobile women in their ranks.

Washington, D.C. (sometimes thought of as the "Federal Government, Inc.") is a city that changes with every new administration. Jobs abound in all areas of law, government, and media, and women's share of managerial and executive jobs is over 43 percent. Downtown D.C. is really a small place, but suburban Silver Spring, Chevy Chase, and Bethesda in Maryland, and Arlington, McLean, and Alexandria in Virginia are all part of Metro D.C. (and are all nice places to live). Metro D.C. still thinks of itself as the South to some extent, and becomes so shocked if it gets a dusting of snow that the airports close for hours!

Also in the Northeast, look at both Pittsburgh and Philadelphia, Pennsylvania, which are growing and offer some new options for women.

In the Southeast, Atlanta tops the list for growth and oportunity for women in an unusual way. The Protestant work ethic never quite took hold in the South, so the region has a very different way of doing business. In almost a Latin American or Far Eastern fashion, "bidness" takes second place in the South to trust and the relationship. Strong patriotic feelings are evident. Turning down a plate of grits can kill a deal, but the business style in the South is full of pleasantries, gentility, and what may seem to those from the East or West to be foot dragging. Not surprisingly, there is a good deal of Japanese investment in the South. A Japanese manufacturer there has said, "We stress the human side of business and so does the South."

Recently, a survey by the University of Florida showed that men and women in the South have moved far from the traditional attitude regarding women, toward acceptance of women who combine work and family obligations. They now view the subject as liberally as people in the Northeast and Midwest (but even more liberal attitudes were found in the West).

Although the Midwest was found to be less favorable in attitude toward working women than any other region in the Texas A&M study, both Chicago and the Minneapolis–St. Paul area provide good alternatives for women who live or want to live in the Midwest. Illinois has an ERA (equal rights amendment), and Chicago is a major cultural center and had a woman mayor, Jane Bryne, a few years ago.

The twin cities, Minneapolis and St. Paul, have a high concentration of businesses with a social conscience. Dayton Hudson, 3M, Control Data, General Mills, and other companies that are concerned with the environment and the quality of work life have their headquarters here.

Negotiating with Americans: A Light-Hearted Guide for the Uninitiated

While I was writing the last few chapters, I had a funny thought: If a woman from overseas were writing about doing business in the United States, what would we sound like to a foreign audience?

If you're in a hurry to get to your next meeting, you can skip the rest of this chapter. But if you can still enjoy a small laugh at your own expense, read on.

The United States is vast in size and influence. The 240 million people who live between the two coasts are three thousand miles apart geographically, and at least that far apart culturally. A New Yorker flying to Los Angeles for a business meeting may be surprised to find that it is being held in a hot tub. It takes almost as long to fly from New York to California as it does to fly to London. On arrival, the culture shock is likely to be extreme in both cases.

The United States is a young, dynamic, and sometimes naive and unsophisticated country. For a person coming from overseas, negotiating with Americans can be a traumatic but ultimately rewarding experience. To begin with, if Americans allow the time for meaningless pleasantries, they will often reveal personal details or ask embarrassing questions. Introductions are fairly standard, complete with business card. Many executives from overseas are astounded to see so many women on the managerial level. These women are usually introduced as Ms. Jane Smith or Ms. Sally Jones and then, as do U.S. businessmen, they will ask to be called by their first name. The pace of negotiation doesn't slacken, and soon the overseas client will be asked to produce a price list, often before having finished the first cup of coffee. This is just as well, considering what American coffee tastes like.

Try to match the U.S. executives' pace to some extent, but if that is too exhausting, slow them down by asking them to talk about their favorite subject: themselves. Americans, particularly New Yorkers, will freely talk about their education since primary school, how much rent they pay, politics, prices, families—almost anything. Don't discuss religion, as the United States is a very diverse society. Stick to a less controversial subject like nuclear disarmament or sex.

Women are in direct competition with men in the United States, and will often match male behavior. Lately, women have begun to interrupt men, correct them when they are wrong (and sometimes when they aren't), and in general, to stand up for themselves. The peculiar habit of women all wearing the same navy blue or grey suit and bow tie is beginning to fade as they become more secure in their own professional identity, but you may still find some women executives dressed as clones of their male colleagues. Do not compliment them on their shade of lipstick.

It is fortunate that most foreign executives speak English, because few Americans speak anything but. Regional accents and rapid speech make most Americans hard to understand, so ask them to slow down politely and they will—for at least a minute. Americans are almost always prompt for a meeting, so don't be surprised if they fuss and fume if you are only 30 minutes late. They have no way of knowing that back home you would be ridiculed for arriving so early. Be patient. When your meeting begins and everyone shakes hands, be certain to step back a bit. Physical proximity makes Americans nervous, and they avoid touching if possible. You need only observe a crowded subway car during rush hour to understand how New Yorkers can be packed like sardines and still avoid touching.

Most Americans are fanatics about personal hygiene. Remember, this is the country that invented deodorant sprays for parts of the body you didn't even know existed. But paradoxically, in many U.S. cities garbage proliferates and people allow their dogs to "foul the footpath."

You may or may not be offered coffee. You do not need to accept, particularly if you dislike the brown liquid served in foam cups that impart a chemical taste, and served with powdered "creme" and sugar that never saw a cow or a cane.

It is usually not necessary to allot more than an hour or two to conduct any business, as Americans are very bottom line–oriented. They want to see a price list, or the final offer, fast. They don't rely on personal relationships in business because they are very mobile. Americans don't need to form a relationship with you because they will probably be at another company the next time you call. They depend on contracts rather than relationships of trust. So, grin and bear it, make the sale or deal, go out for a "leisurely" 20-minute lunch with your client, and move on to your next appointment.

10

The International Businesswoman at Home: Working in the United States for a Foreign Firm

In the preface to my first book, I noted that you don't need to travel overseas to use this book because international business is being conducted every day right here in the United States. That was written in 1985. This is even more true today, due to the recent surge of acquisitions of U.S. businesses by foreign owners. Last year you worked for CBS; today you're working for a wholly owned subsidiary of Sony. Last month you worked for Pillsbury; today you're under the management of a British conglomerate called Grand Metropolitan PLC, so goodbye "Doughboy." Last week you were at First Boston advising your U.S. corporate clients on takeovers and mergers. This week, First Boston itself was taken over by Credit Suisse.

In deals worth millions—and sometimes billions—of U.S. dollars, companies are merging with, being taken over by, and being invested in by foreign corporations in record numbers. The controversy over whether we're selling the United States "on the cheap" or receiving healthy infusions of cash rages on. Nevertheless, the acquisition of U.S. companies by foreign (and other domestic) companies continues with no end in sight. It is another indication of how industry is being increasingly globalized and how national boundaries seem to be breaking down.

In 1988, Japanese direct investment in U.S. companies beat out the traditional investment leaders, Britain and the Netherlands, for the first time. But the British still have a 29 percent share of total direct investment in the United States, compared with a 16 percent share for the Japanese.

The Japanese are also becoming more active in corporate acquisitions. In a strange twist, Japanese securities professionals are being taught the wild and wooly acquisitions game, a uniquely U.S. business, by U.S. mergers and acquisitions companies. The Blackstone Group, Wasserstein Perella and Company, and the Lodestar Group, all partially acquired by Japanese companies recently, have brought in Japanese trainees to learn the culture of U.S. takeovers.

Foreign investors have found U.S. securities and financial service firms particularly attractive. Nearly all the giants of Wall Street now have at least minority foreign ownership: Goldman Sachs, Paine Webber, and Shearson Lehman are partly owned by Japanese companies; a South African concern is a minority owner of Salomon Brothers; and a consortium of Middle Eastern investors is a minority owner of Smith Barney. Similarly, foreign investors have acquired many U.S. banks; for example, California First Bank and Crocker Bank are both now British-owned. Insurance companies have also been a popular target for foreign investors.

This trend, however, is not limited to the financial services field. For example, European investors are acquiring U.S. supermarket chains: Grand Union is now owned by a French company, and A&P by a German concern.

Some of the other areas in which foreign companies have invested heavily or acquired include media (Doubleday, the publishing giant, is now German-owned), consumer products, especially health and beauty aids, and real estate. Hundreds of office buildings, apartment complexes, and hotels throughout all parts of the United States are owned by foreign investors. Interestingly, these are all industries in which women have long had a strong presence. Women began in low-level positions in these areas 20 years ago, and in many cases have risen toward senior management. What a perfect opportunity for the woman in these industries who wants to work for a foreign company right here in the United States!

Although the pace of foreign acquisitions of U.S. companies has increased in recent years, the phenomenon is hardly a new one. As a child growing up in the United States in the ultra patriotic decade of the 1950s, I was dismayed to discover that Nestles, the maker of my favorite candy bar, was a Swiss rather than a U.S. company. I imagine my father would have been equally surprised to learn that *his* favorite treat, Seagram's Seven Crown, was made by a Canadian distiller.

To this day, when I give seminars on international business, my attendees often gasp when they learn that such household-name companies as Lever Brothers and Shell Oil are not American but Dutch; that Prudential Corp. is British; and that New York's venerable Algonquin Hotel is now Japanese.

While the management of partially foreign-owned companies is not radically changing the U.S. status quo and management style that exists, some acquired companies are being revitalized. A top executive at Japan's CBS-Sony said "Sony is committed to long term development. We did not get that kind of commitment from CBS."

On the other hand, there is often a lack of commitment to promoting and nurturing executive women in Japanese-owned companies. Japanese companies often export their country's national attitudes to the United States. And sometimes U.S. companies that zealously seek foreign investment do not inform the foreign investor about U.S. labor and equal opportunity laws. The ten years of class action litigation between Sumitomo and 13 female secretaries and clerical workers charging discriminatory hiring practices was settled in 1987 when the company agreed to spend $2.8 million to train, promote, and better pay its female workers.

Honda of America Manufacturing, Inc., also recently settled an Equal Employment Opportunity Commission (EEOC) case charging sexual discrimination, and similar lawsuits are pending against the U.S. officers of several other large Japanese companies. In some cases these firms are being charged with discriminating not only against women, but also against men of non-Asian ancestry.

Japanese management in the United States apparently isn't strongly committed to the advancement of U.S. *men's* careers either. According to a *Business Week* article that surveyed Japanese operations throughout the United States, "American managers are beginning to feel like second class citizens in Japanese companies." This had led to difficulties for some Japanese firms' efforts to penetrate U.S. markets. For example, the "Big Four" securities firms of Japan—Nomura, Daiwa, Yamaichi, and Nikko—have made little progress in their attempts to crack the Wall Street market, a trend that many attribute to their failure to attract qualified U.S. employees.

On the other hand, some Japanese firms are making efforts to attract and promote U.S. executives, but only a few success stories exist to date. In March 1989, Matsushita named an American as president and CEO of its U.S. unit. The rise of the highly regarded Richard Kraft is seen as an effort to diffuse criticism that Japanese companies rarely give foreigners key jobs. He said his selection was all the more amazing because he doesn't play tennis or golf, two favorite pastimes of Japanese executives!

Many wholly Japanese–owned companies operating in the United States are beginning to recruit U.S. managers, in part because it is more practical than importing executives from Japan, and partly in the hope that an American face will make for easier business dealings. This trend bodes well for women managers in these companies.

Aside from Japanese companies, there are many foreign companies that, even if they are not as committed to promoting women as are U.S. companies, certainly hold strong potential for women. Louise Gunderson was hired away from a successful and visible post at Chemical Bank by Banca della Svizzera Italiana, the sixth largest commercial bank in Switzerland, to head up a new U.S. private-banking unit. She was hired because, according to the (male) CEO of the bank: "In hiring Mrs. Gunderson and her group, we are trying to get U.S. clients. It is difficult for a foreign bank to do that in the U.S." Japanese companies would do well to heed that advice. Many foreign companies are learning to look beyond gender and toward an individual's ability to contribute to the bottom line. Acceptance of high-level women in management is still slow, but the ability of a person to produce profits is becoming more important than whether the person who produces wears a skirt or trousers.

Once again, women's natural style of doing business can be most useful when seeking opportunities in foreign-owned companies. A U.S. woman has the management expertise garnered from working in the United States combined with the more patient, flexible, and team-oriented style that is so common to American women and so necessary for success in international business.

Although you may need to overcome some management resistance to the fact of being female, don't hesitate to quietly and diplomatically demonstrate your abilities. Above all, know everything about the industry and the company you want to work for because as a woman you'll be held up to closer scrutiny. Do everything twice as well as a man, be firm but not aggressive, and show knowledge of and respect for the foreign culture. But that's how you've been successful with your U.S. employer anyway, so go out and "be global."

At the same time that foreign investors are buying U.S. firms, there is a new surge of investment overseas by American companies seeking to further "globalize." This trend is providing new opportunities for U.S. men and women to work abroad, especially in Europe and Asia where consumer markets are booming. The long-term trend appears to be away from exports and toward operating and manufacturing inside the foreign market. U.S. companies invested over $42 billion in plants and equipment overseas in 1988. In anticipation of the 1992 consolidation of Europe, U.S. acquisitions there tripled in one year from $1.3 billion in 1987 to $3.6 billion in 1988. Although many of these U.S. companies hire workers in the host country, the overall growth from this expansion also provides many opportunities for Americans in providing ancillary services. Strategic marketing planning, market research, public relations, operations, product design, and hundreds of other functions and industries based in the United States benefit from increased overseas investment.

Even those U.S. firms that have not invested in overseas plants are finding increased international opportunities. U.S. exports such as toys, crackers and cookies, toiletries and cosmetics, and other consumer goods have enjoyed a resurgence in demand in the past year. Opportunities to travel overseas or to accept a foreign posting for that all-important overseas experience are on the upswing. Soon globalization won't just be a glamorous word, but a means for the United States to once more become the economic engine driving the world.

11

Breaking Down Barriers: Nine Stories

Woman are receiving assignments overseas in increasing numbers. However, the reception they get on arrival varies greatly. Even within the same country, a woman may be accepted easily in one city and treated rudely in another. Often, the further away from Europe you go, the more difficult it becomes to be accepted. Nonetheless, women have and will continue to conduct business successfully, even in remote and unusual places throughout the world.

Women come to careers in international business in different ways, and from different backgrounds. In this chapter, I tell the stories of nine women who have all succeeded in international business, each in her own way. These women began their careers in varying fields—domestic business, languages, government, even filmmaking. But all of them learned the ways to do business successfully with clients who come from other countries and cultures.

Linda Pakh, vice president, Bank of New York, was a Russian-language major in college. She spent a semester at Leningrad University where she met her husband, the son of a Russian mother and a Hungarian father. Linda lived in Budapest for a year, and then returned to New York where she got a job as a tour escort. She then traveled for a year, leading tour groups to Siberia, Tashkent, Kiev, Odessa, and Moscow.

Soon after, Linda got a new job as an interpreter for the U.S. architectural firm that designed the Moscow World Trade Center. She bluffed her way into the job by saying she was fluent in Russian technical terms and could type in Cyrillic (the Russian alphabet) as well. She succeeded as a translator, and next moved on to an administrative job at the U.S.-Yugoslav Economic Council. During that time, Linda studied for her MBA at night.

She was soon hired by The Bank of New York and participated in a credit training program. Her first assignment was working with the correspondent banks in Eastern Europe. One day Linda found herself negotiating alone at a meeting in Yugoslavia with a group of Yugoslav businessmen. They were discussing the interest rate they'd be willing to pay on a loan. The Yugoslavs lapsed into Serbo-Croatian (a language similar to Russian), not realizing that Linda could understand them. She was able to ascertain their true bottom-line price, and negotiated the loan on terms highly favorable to her bank. Linda went on to negotiate loans in Budapest, Bucharest, Prague, Warsaw, Moscow, and East Berlin. She found her Eastern European clients to be far less sophisticated about banking than their Western European counterparts. She held their hands and educated them about the bank's products and how to make deals, becoming their friend and advisor.

Linda found that to do business anywhere in Eastern Europe, you must be prepared to socialize with your clients and develop personal relationships. Although she came to love the Eastern Europeans for their warmth, their genuine love and admiration of women, and their unsophisticated charm, she kissed the ground every time she returned to the West. Linda today prefers the faster-paced, more sophisticated business culture of the United States and Canada, but freely admits that she owes her success to her international experience.

Barbara Stewart, an investment manager, has traveled to the Middle East a number of times. She has successfully conducted business in Saudi Arabia, Tunisia, Jordan, Iraq, and Egypt. While doing business is vastly different in Egypt than it is in Saudi Arabia, Barbara feels that "if they want your product and you are professional they will accept you anywhere in the Middle East."

She thinks her success is based on understanding how the society works and knowing what to expect. Barbara explained that while men have an easier entry into Saudi Arabia, they must have contacts already established just as a woman must. No one can expect to get to Saudi Arabia and then make phone calls to set up appointments. This must all be prearranged, and channels of communication must be established in advance. Barbara doesn't mind the restrictions placed on women in Saudi Arabia. She'd rather stay as a guest of a Saudi family than at the Hilton, and prefers a ride on a segregated bus to New York City subways. Even as a Westerner, the official and informal rules that restrict the freedom of Arab women were applied to her. (This is true, however, primarily in Saudi Arabia, and only rarely in other Arab countries.)

She didn't mind wearing long sleeves and a long skirt. "It's not terribly different from my old New York uniform of dark blue suit, long sleeve blouse and low heel pumps," she added.

Barbara met a number of Saudi women who are doing business. However, women in Saudi Arabia may do business only with other women. Many of these businesses are fairly large in size. Women in Saudi Arabia have their own bank as well. She noted that a good deal of money is controlled by women in Saudi Arabia, and in other countries in the Middle East as well. Saudi women, however, are extremely restricted professionally. They are only allowed into a handful of professions, including teaching at a segregated school and writing for the women's section of a newspaper. Many of the young women seem to defend the restrictions placed on them. Barbara Stewart believes that many of them have been influenced by the recent resurgence of Islamic fundamentalism.

In Egypt, women often work side by side with men, and rarely wear the veil. Women socialize with men, and many are involved in the arts. Barbara enjoyed the relaxed tolerance in Egypt. While the country is basically conservative, in Cairo and Alexandria there are no restrictions on business interactions with women.

In Amman, Jordan, things are somewhat similar. Again, Barbara could hardly wear jogging shorts, but she was free to move about anywhere on her own, and even to have dinner alone at a restaurant. Now married, Barbara traveled to the Middle East while she was still single. In some places she invented a husband in order to forestall any questions about her personal life from both men and women. However, she was often questioned about her husband's feelings about her travels. She now explains truthfully that he doesn't mind since she is only away for a few weeks at a time. Barbara said that after the first few times, it became like traveling for business in any other place in the world: exhilarating, but exhausting.

Diane Simpson, president of Simpson International Inc., a small, New York-based management consulting firm specializing in U.S.-Japanese business, began her career as an academic psychologist.

After she and her husband got their Ph.D.s in 1969, they decided to see the world before settling down to teach in the United States. Her husband had been interested in Japan ever since his sixth grade geography project, so they went to Japan, where she took a research position in the psychology department of Japan's Sophia University. She decided against teaching in English and doing essentially what she would have been doing in the United States, so she learned Japanese and became a consultant to the Japanese Psychological Association.

When Diane and her husband moved to New York, she wanted to put her hard-won proficiency in Japanese language and culture to work in the business world, but she had no business experience. So she spent the next year reading *Business Week*, the *Wall Street Journal*, and any business publications she could get her hands on. In 1981, she found a job through an employment agency with Nomura Securities International, the first Japanese member firm of the New York Stock Exchange. Diane was hired as executive assistant to the president of Nomura's U.S. subsidiary. Shortly thereafter, he asked her to participate with him at an International Monetary Fund conference in Washington, D.C. At the conference, she attended a dinner with nine high-ranking Japanese males, including her boss and his supervisor, the president of Nomura's Japanese parent company.

Diane's boss praised her abilities to the Japanese president, who then turned to her and said, "What I want to know is, how many children do you have?" When Diane replied that she had none, the senior official replied "Any woman who does not have at least 10 children, has no right to call herself a woman."

Even with her deep understanding of Japanese culture, Diane was shocked to hear such a blunt statement of what he really thought. Her boss seemed surprised too, but nevertheless continued to support her career, and even sent her to high-level Nomura training programs.

In 1985, Diane's boss suggested that she leave Nomura before he did so he could continue to be of help to her. She became a consultant to various subsidiaries of Nomura, and started Simpson International. Through her former boss, she was introduced to many Japanese and American companies, which eventually became her clients.

With her Japanese business contacts, Diane has found that she is perceived as a foreigner first, as an experienced and mature executive second, and as a female only third. Because of her fluency in Japanese, she is able to control the perception of her gender by using the neutral rather than feminine form of speech. Diane attributes her success to hard work and in-depth knowledge of her customers and markets, which can only be acquired through experience.

Eugenia Thackeray, a senior-level U.S. government public relations officer, traveled widely in the Far East and was posted in Indonesia for three years. She felt that it took her a year to acclimate to her surroundings and to think less like an American. Eugenia said that one of the biggest differences between Asia and the West is the importance of tranquility. In most Western societies, noise, motion, and agitation abound, both publicly and privately. For Asians, however, nothing is more desired than tranquility and quiet. A low, calm, soft voice will get peoples' attention much more quickly than abrasive shouting.

Genie said that the Far East differs from the United States particularly in the level of formality. Asians are rarely casual the way people are in the West. For example, it is unthinkable to sit in a chair or sofa sprawled out American style.

Throughout Asia, personal contacts count for everything. Eugenia explained that it took a while for her to be accepted by the Indonesians; her Indonesian counterparts who worked at the U.S. installation were the contacts that helped her break the barriers. They introduced her to key people and gave her entree to Indonesian society. She spent a lot of time chatting about the loveliness of Indonesia before she was able to begin doing business. Eugenia learned that usually she could not come directly to the point. If time was pressing and she felt the need to speed up the pace of the discussion, she would say, "May I be terribly American?"

As she was accepted into Indonesian society she began to be invited to weddings and parties, and learned to converse in an indirect style with everyone she met. She discussed trips, families, and food, but always in an impersonal manner. Genie had to revise her thinking in order to speak about personal things impersonally. She invited all she met to visit the United States, and never, ever said anything critical about Indonesia. She pointed out that in Asia you must never lose face or embarrass other people by asking questions they don't want to answer.

In negotiating a price for a seminar, Eugenia discovered that in Indonesia prices are never firm. In the United States for the most part our price is the figure on the price list. Most U.S.-to-U.S. business is done based on that price and only occasionally is the price bargained down. In Indonesia, however, as in many other parts of the world, any price is considered negotiable.

Bribes are part of the Asian social structure as well. Genie Thackeray had to suppress her distaste and accept totally different values. One highly prized way to thank someone for a favor is to give a small wrapped gift, with a "made in the United States" label clearly in sight. Despite this unpleasant practice, Eugenia came to enjoy the different customs of Indonesia and found it somewhat difficult to readjust to the "boorish" attitude of U.S. business.

Ursula Stevens, director of imports/exports at Sun Chemical Corporation, is one of the highest-ranking women in the almost totally male-dominated specialty chemical industry. She was born in a small village outside of Stuttgart, Germany, and came to the United States in 1959 at the age of 20. Ursula spoke no English when she arrived here, and had only the equivalent of an 11th grade education and some accounting skills. Her first jobs were at a knitwear factory and a bakery.

Later, as her English improved, she got a clerical job in the admitting office of a hospital. Within seven years of coming to the United States, Ursula had worked her way up to the position of credit manager at a Sears branch. Soon after that, she moved to Rutherford, New Jersey, and got a job with Sun Chemical. Although she started with Sun as a typist, she quickly advanced through a variety of positions, eventually becoming office manager. Then, in 1973, Ursula became controller of Sun's international division.

Rushing to her desk early every morning, Ursula took a shortcut through the plant floor. She became fascinated by the heavy machinery used to print colorful logos directly onto metal cans. She soon began to learn everything she could about Sun Chemical's inks and their applications. By the time she was sent on a sales trip to Continental Can, she knew everything about her product.

By 1975, Ursula was going on business trips to Sun's overseas subsidiaries. Visiting the European subsidiaries in particular felt like going home for her. Although many clients were initially surprised to see a woman in this high-level position, Sun Chemical firmly backed up her recommendations. Senior managers of the company had confidence in her knowledge and trusted her to assist the subsidiaries (or subs) in expanding their business. In turn, the managers of the subs came to recognize her importance to the company and ultimately accepted her authority.

Today, as director of the entire import/export division of Sun Chemical Corporation, Ursula emphasizes the importance of technical expertise for any woman trying to overcome resistance from male middle managers. "Learning the business from the bottom up was crucial to my success," says Ursula. "When you know what you're talking about better than anyone else, upper management will have to give you their support."

Noelle Johnson had no prior experience in dealing with the Japanese until she was given a gift by a friend who had spent some time in Japan. Noelle, an artist, was particularly impressed with the gift, which used a proprietary process that would transfer designs onto ceramic. She thought that the kits would make excellent gifts for do-it-yourselfers who were interested in making pottery.

Noelle did some research and learned the name of the manufacturer. She wrote him a letter explaining her interest in importing and setting up channels of distribution for the product. In turn, she received a letter saying that the manufacturer, Mr. Ishikowa, was seeking a distributor network in the United States. She began a six-month period of letter writing and telephoning. Fortunately, Mr. Ishikowa was fairly fluent in English. While he seemed surprised to hear that Noelle Johnson was a woman, he was still receptive to her. She spoke very softly and made oblique suggestions and references to what she wanted without asking for anything. She allowed Mr. Ishikowa to come to the conclusion that she might be the best person to represent his product in the United States. Noelle expressed such genuine interest in the product that Mr. Ishikowa began to trust her. When she suggested that she come to Japan to meet the inventor of the process, he was completely won over.

Mr. Ishikowa was enthusiastic about her forthcoming trip. He promised to make introductions for her, teach her more about the pottery and ceramic business, and in general show her a little bit about how business is conducted in Japan. She spent the next month reading every book about Japan that she could find. She learned bowing protocol, eating habits, and as much about Japanese culture as possible. She also learned a few phrases in Japanese, a skill that would ease the awkwardness of many situations.

Mr. Ishikowa was true to his word, and taught her the ceramic pottery process in a few weeks. He introduced her to the elderly inventor of the design-transfer device. During this time, Noelle did not even mention the possibility of representing the process in the United States. She simply learned all she was taught, made suggestions, and was thoroughly appreciative. Mr. Ishikowa and the inventor were thrilled with her professional ability and involvement. She even made suggestions about names for the kit that would be marketable in the United States.

She went back to the United States and spoke to Mr. Ishikowa every two weeks. After six months, Noelle felt the need for more training in the process, and at the urging of Mr. Ishikowa went back to Japan. Mr. Ishikowa told her that, unknown to her, he already had a distributor for his company in the United States. She didn't act shocked, but rather told Mr. Ishikowa that she could help train the representative in the process. Mr. Ishikowa thought it would be an excellent idea. Noelle went back to New York and met with the distributor, who told her he wanted Mr. Ishikowa's other product lines but didn't want this particular product. She telexed Japan, and said, "Let me represent your excellent product, since the distributor doesn't want it." Mr. Ishikowa gave her one year. She asked politely for a contract, and he explained that it is unnecessary in Japan. Noelle explained that in the U.S. market it was absolutely necessary that she have written proof that she was the rep, and Mr. Ishikowa agreed.

Early the next year she took the product to a trade show in which 600 companies participated. Interest was high, but she learned that the packaging and instructions had to be changed for the U.S. market. She asked Mr. Ishikowa for more time, and he said she could have two more years.

After a few months a major company became interested in the product. Noelle got a contract on a commission deal. She was now the official manufacturer's U.S. representative for "Floramika." Her perseverance, belief in the product, and respect for the Japanese way of doing business enabled Noelle Johnson to succeed.

In 1981, *Jane Altschuler* (now president of Jane Altschuler Productions) was already running a film production company. She had produced and directed television spots and industrial films, but had never made a film outside the United States.

In 1981, Jane met a member of the Joint Agricultural Consultative Committee (JACC), a group working to improve trade between the United States and Nigeria. Nigeria, the leading oil producer in Africa, had an $11-billion trade surplus with the United States in 1981, but its economy outside the oil sector was underdeveloped. Nigeria's government, then experimenting with democracy, was eager to improve its relationship with the United States.

The JACC was headed up by then vice president George Bush, and included senior executives of Mobil, Chrysler, Ford, and other U.S.

companies operating in Africa as well as top Nigerian businessmen. Through Jane's contact at JACC, she was commissioned to make a film to educate the American people about the progress being made in Nigeria.

Jane assembled a team of seven high-quality cameramen and technicians. But when she arrived in Nigeria, local officials insisted that she include a well-known Nigerian actor/filmmaker on her team. Jane was initially dubious, feeling that he added nothing to the crew she had so carefully assembled. But as they began traveling around the country, she found that his presence was essential in obtaining the support and cooperation of the people and the local officials, even though she had been given a triple-A clearance by the Nigerian government. Jane found that the only way to get things done in Nigeria was to show respect for Nigerian customs, and to allow her hosts to make arrangements for her and her team.

When Jane was scheduled to film the Nigerian House and Senate in session, the senators saw the white cameramen and crew setting up their equipment and refused to let them film. Jane dismised her crew and spoke privately to the officials. She began by greeting them in Hausa, the local language, and immediately gained their trust by showing her interest in their culture. Having broken down their initial resistance, she continued in English and respectfully explained how important it was to Nigeria for Americans to learn about Nigeria's people and institutions. Jane was graciously allowed to complete her film. *Nigeria: The Unknown Giant.*

Pat Winters, 24 years old, was told by her boss-to-be during her interviews for a sales position that would possibly include overseas travel that she would have to work extra hard to be taken seriously because she was young and attractive. She swallowed her anger and took the job. She has traveled widely throughout Europe and has had a few problems being taken seriously by her overseas clients. The ambiguity of her name suggested to her European clients (who had only corresponded with her) that she might be male. Her clients were quite surprised to meet her at first, but her knowledge of the countries, the cultures, and the products she was selling quickly became apparent.

During her recent trip to the United Kingdom, Norway, France, West Germany, and Italy, her clients were impressed at the extent of her product knowledge. She firmly believes it is this understanding of what she sells, her belief in those products, and her enthusiasm for them that makes the age/sex issue less of a barrier.

My own experience as a marketing consultant centers mainly around

Latin America, Europe, and the Far East. Prior nonbusiness experience in Latin America and a good command of the Spanish language gave me tremendous insight into a somewhat difficult-to-penetrate business climate. Only ten years ago, in 1980, when I attended an industrial fair in Bogotá, Colombia, I was one of the few professional women present. Of course, there were the ubiquitous glamorous models draped over the stands and equipment, but otherwise there were no other women attendees or exhibitors. While trade fairs, even in the United States, always seem to bring out the worst in attendees (who are usually men far from home), this particular fair was made less than pleasant for me because of the unwarranted (and unwanted) attention I received. At meetings things were somewhat easier, and as the carnival atmosphere of the trade show began to fade after the opening festivities, it became easier to be accepted as a professional. It was obvious that the Colombians and other Latin Americans at the show were not used to seeing, much less dealing with, U.S. businesswomen. During the course of the next few years a fair number of U.S. women began traveling to Latin America to do business, and it became easier to be accepted.

Before the debt crisis exploded in the early part of 1982, I had been contracted to do a cost reduction and marketing feasibility study for a large corporation in Mexico City. This was during the time that the Mexican government and corporations were borrowing cash and spending it freely. Many companies were engaged in building conglomerates by all forms of merger and acquisition. In both Mexico City and Monterrey, MBAs from the United States were being courted like royalty. It became part of the corporate growth imperative to have MBA consultants as part of the team. Most people thought that the oil boom and business expansion were permanent features of the Mexican economy. Traditional Mexican resentment toward the United States began to diminish as prosperity seemed near. Nevertheless, Mexican managers were not used to having U.S. women map out acquisition strategies, marketing plans, or cost-reduction programs. I was treated politely by lower management, but certainly not welcomed. After the first few days of going over the objectives with the English-speaking senior manager, I began to wonder why lower management seemed resistant to my overtures. While I knew that many of the men spoke English, I used my carefully practiced Spanish with them. My recommendations and plans were to be written in English and then translated into Spanish. When I used English with the men, few of them responded. I began to feel frustrated and afraid that I couldn't get enough cooperation to successfully complete my work. One Friday, a group of managers and administrative assistants (one female) were talking about their plans for the weekend. One of the men said in very rapid and slangy Mexican Spanish, "Let's get the hell out of here and have a big blowout tonight." Without thinking, I asked if I could join them, or if the party was only for the "machos." Their surprise that I knew the slangy local connotation of "blow-out" (*reventon* in Spanish) was obvious. They were delighted that I spoke their language and said that of course I could join them.

As I got to know the men individually, they loosened up considerably. I made it very clear to all concerned that I had deep respect for and interest in the culture and future well-being of Mexico. In many instances I asked for their "expert" opinion even when I knew the answer. It was a constructive way of showing my involvement with them rather than just with the procedures at hand.

The men I worked with had an insatiable thirst for consumer products from the United States, but an ambivalent attitude toward the American people. Many Mexicans are convinced that U.S. goods are superior to those manufactured in Mexico and proudly show off their U.S. purchases, while at the same time expressing angry feelings toward U.S. "imperialist policy." This explains the ambivalence toward consultants from the United States. I was able to overcome much ill-feeling by showing that I like and respect the Mexican culture enough to study it and incorporate it into my way of doing business.

One of the first times I went to Brazil, I met with government, bank, and trade association officials. I was anxious at first because my Portuguese was poor. I was delighted to learn, during my many meetings, that in Rio de Janeiro and São Paulo, English is often the language of international business. Quite unlike Mexico, Brazil has a positive, mostly nonambivalent admiration for the United States. Perhaps the sheer size of the country or its distance from the United States is responsible. While few of the offices I visited had women staff members other than secretaries, one of the main exporters' associations had a well-educated professional woman as the assistant to the president.

At each meeting I was offered a cup of the thick, strong coffee for which Brazil is so famous, always served black, along with a glass of ice water. I accepted each time. By the end of the day, I had drunk enough coffee to float home, but I never refused a cup nor neglected to comment on the exquisite flavor.

Although I had corresponded with the people I met for weeks beforehand, I spent a good deal of time talking about the beauty of the local scenery, the gentility of the people, and the economic progress that had been made. My clients spoke English in varying degrees but were all anxious to practice it with me. I encouraged them, wishing I could speak Portuguese as well. In many instances, English is the second language studied at school, and in some Brazilian schools studying English is mandatory.

Brazilians are for the most part an agreeable, pleasant, and intelligent people. The meetings had a fairly slow pace in Rio de Janeiro and a more pressured quality in São Paulo. There were more women in lower-management in the offices of my clients in São Paulo, but still not many overall. The climate is also somewhat more conducive to business in temperate São Paulo than in tropical Rio. One of my business lunches in Rio in a huge old club-like building lasted for almost three hours. In São Paulo lunch was an affair of a little over an hour in a slick glass and chrome nouvelle cuisine restaurant, where my client apologized for the slow service.

My meetings in Rio were primarily intended to set the stage for future dealings in the areas of import/export and countertrade (a form of barter), and were very successful. Because I sincerely showed that I wanted to begin a long-term commercial relationship with Brazilian companies and agencies, appointments were set up for me with various Brazilian branch offices in the United States. My relationships with some of my clients continue to this day.

I saw just how comfortable Paulistas (residents of São Paulo) are doing business with women when I was invited back to Brazil last year. IBOPE, the largest and most respected Brazilian market research firm, which is headquartered in São Paulo, asked me to deliver a seminar on marketing trends of the 1990s. The directors of IBOPE notified the press, and perhaps because a high-level woman is still something of a novelty in Brazil, I woke up each morning to see my picture on the front page of the business section of many of Brazil's leading newspapers.

My audience at the seminar, which was aimed at mid- to high-level marketing professionals, included about 80 men and 15 women. IBOPE handed out copies of the first edition of this book to all the participants. It was a joy to see so many men proudly clutching *The International Businesswomen*, something no man except my husband would do in the United States!

In a business trip to England a few years ago, I had the opportunity to meet with a group of United Kingdom business and professional women, who were hosting a party for a visiting group of executives from New York's Financial Women's Association (FWA). (The FWA women were being feted for a week by various British hosts and groups.) Fortunately, I was on assignment in London during the time of the receptions, and as an FWA member, I was invited to participate. While there were exceptions, the majority of the British women were somewhat older and less educated than their New York counterparts. Many of the British women were owners of their own businesses. There are few women at the level of manager and above in most British corporations.

One reception was held by the young members of the all-male London Bond Club for the bankers, lawyers, and managers that make up the membership of the Financial Women's Association. When asked to comment on the incidence of women in business and professional capacities in the United Kingdom, one member remarked that "We have a few women like you [FWA] but we're really just beginning to see them." Another fellow, good-naturedly overwhelmed by the biographical histories of the FWA members, said to me upon being introduced, "Oh my God, are you another financial vice president?" Nevertheless, the admiration for the FWA membership was evident.

My clients in London were of long-standing so there was no need for a lengthy getting-to-know-you period. They are the top management of a large, sophisticated corporation with branch offices in the United States, and had dealt extensively with women managers.

My attendance at a trade show was somewhat less enjoyable. Few women attended, and fewer exhibited. In all fairness, however, U.K. industrial trade shows are pretty much the same as those in the United States, where there are still few women present except at computer-related shows. (Computers are a fairly new industry, so women have a relatively higher profile.) Regarding high-level executive women, the United Kingdom still seems to be where the United States was roughly 10 to 15 years ago.

Although equality for women may be far off in many parts of the world, there is almost no country in which a woman executive from the United States cannot succeed if she is patient, prepared, and professional.

12

Global Marketing

If half the formula for success overseas is to know all you can about your client's market, the other half is to know how to sell in that market. This means you have to know the people with whom you'll be dealing; and you have to know how to present your product or service to the country to which you'll be selling. The first step is to learn everything about your product, service, or deal. The women who are most succesful are the ones who, in addition to learning cultural norms, take the time to become expert in their field. Superficial knowledge of what you're peddling isn't enough in the competitive world market. Many clients know a great deal more about your products or services than you may think. You must be prepared to field the most obscure questions about specifications, payment, performance, warranty, and contractual obligations—for starters.

But no matter how much you know, in many parts of the world it is also essential to have at least one local partner on your team. If you are negotiating for a large contract or attempting to enter a major new market, this could be the best, fastest, and often the only way to succeed. This partner is the key to market intelligence that may be unavailable through traditional market research efforts. "You can *buy* in any language," writes Robert Carothers of Minnesota State University, but "you *sell* in the language of the customer."

In Asia, entering into a business agreement has been likened to joining a family. With a careful investigation of the ethics and financial abilities of your potential partner, you can become a presence in the Asian market in a fairly short time. If you are selling consumer products or services, having an Asian partner or advisor can be invaluable. Asian tastes are often very far from what Americans think is attractive, palatable, or useful.

For example, except when selling to upscale teenagers in Japan, goods or services that reflect the U.S. obsession with youth are probably less marketable in Asian societies that admire the wisdom that comes with age. This, of course, is an obvious difference. There are also many subtle differences in consumer behavior that few U.S. businesspeople know about.

Having a partner is not only a shortcut to market entry and a source of market intelligence, but in the Arab world it is probably the only way to negotiate a large project. Negotiations in the Middle East also take a good deal of time. Although women can be very successful, it certainly helps (for both men and women) to have an Arab partner on your team. If your company is interested in establishing a presence in the Arab world, you must be prepared to put up with the peculiarities of doing business there. Who else but a local partner would know if the product's packaging or ad campaign are politically sensitive or offend a Moslem religious practice.

A local partner need not be a major stockholder in your company. Instead, a reputable firm or individual can be hired on a project, contingency, percentage, or per diem basis. Think of the difference a local marketing research firm would have made to a U.S. canned soup company which bombed in certain Latin American countries. They could have told the manufacturer that a packaged bouillon cube sold as a soup starter allowed traditional women to feel they were cooking something nutritious for their families, whereas canned soup didn't feel "cooked" to these women. The European manufacturer of powdered and cubed soup bases is still doing very well, while the U.S. company lost a great deal of money and withdrew from the market.

There has been a good deal of debate over the validity of "global goods," which are sold everywhere with the same formula and packaging. While there is great similarity in consumer tastes in the major urban centers of the world, less than 20 percent of the population of the developing world lives in these urban areas. Two-thirds of the world's total population is found in the developing countries. So while global brands certainly have a place outside the developed world, they are somewhat limited to cosmopolitan centers such as São Paulo, Lagos, Cairo, and Seoul. It is in these great centers that the homogenizing effects of media and money have created global markets. Electric typewriters, frozen dinners, and designer cookies probably won't find a large market in most of the Sudan.

Global marketing strategies tend to work fairly well with mature low-cost items such as soft drinks, cosmetics, transistor radios, cigarettes, and jeans. The most famous examples of these are Marlboro and Coca-Cola. At the other end of the spectrum, high-priced items can also often be sold with a global campaign. Diamonds, expensive scotch, and top-of-the-line automobiles often use a fairly standard approach in their marketing.

While global marketing and advertising save a great deal of money by standardization, it is dangerous to attempt to sell most products or services on a global basis. Global marketing usually includes global advertising: one basic campaign is used throughout the world. But many countries have strict prohibitions on certain forms of advertising, which may interfere with a global marketing strategy. For example, in the United Kingdom even the Marlboro cowboy has been prohibited. Government health officials feel it is dangerous to show heroic figures in cigarette ads because they might encourage people to smoke.

In many countries, comparative claims in advertising aren't allowed; in some, children are not permitted to endorse products on television. Of course, there has been an almost worldwide push to restrict advertising of cigarettes, liquor, violent toys, and some over-the-counter drugs in all media.

Obviously, though, the greatest problem with global marketing is the cultural difference between people. While shampoo is pretty much shampoo throughout the world, the advertiser must be sure that racial and ethnic differences, time, locale, and regional preferences are all taken into consideration. An ad showing a blonde-haired model washing her hair at night with shampoo smelling of carnations might bomb miserably in an Asian country where the women all have dark hair and wash their hair in the morning, and where carnations are associated with death and mourning.

One area where global marketing *has* worked is entertainment; U.S. popular music, television shows, and movies are in demand almost everywhere around the world. As one analyst has explained, "American culture is the only true mass worldwide culture."

Perhaps the reason that global marketing has been so successful for media, soft drinks, and jeans, is that these products are consumed primarily by young people. No matter how great the cultural differences between countries, there is clearly a universal youth culture emerging among teenagers throughout the world. Walk the streets of Tokyo, Munich, São Paulo, Chicago, or Tel Aviv, and you'll find teenagers dressed the same, listening to the same pop music, and drinking Coke. The importance of learning to sell to this "global teenager" cannot be underestimated: This year (1990) close to 30 percent of the world's population (almost 1.4 billion people) will be between the ages of 10 and 20.

Global marketing is more difficult for services than for consumer goods. Law and accounting firms must research their markets very carefully to determine the extent of litigation, the tax structure, and the financial reporting procedures of each country in order to fit their services to that country. In fact, in some countries foreigners are completely barred from rendering legal, accounting, medical, and other professional services. Other countries permit foreign professionals to practice only if they pass a local licensing examination and if the local licensing officials approve their foreign degrees. Banks and other financial service companies must understand the makeup of the savings, loan, and investment market in relation to consumer behavior.

Whatever type of company you represent, whether it deals in consumer goods, services, or industrial projects or products, you cannot over-research your market. The object of your research is to avoid all the costly blunders that have become a part of marketing history and folklore: Selling women's razors in the European countries where women don't shave, pushing deodorant to men in countries like Italy and the Philippines where only a small percentage of men use it, offering things in packages of four in Japan where four is the number of death, selling door mats to wipe shoes in Japan where people remove their shoes before entering their homes, or using an ad showing a solitary woman making a major purchase in countries where the traditional family structure is still powerful.

Once you know your product and have researched the culture of your target market, you will be able to tell if there is a proper fit. If you are not sure of a fit, you may have to adapt your goods or services to the culture. Very often this can be accomplished by minor modifications.

There are many countries in the world where products must be changed to conform to the legal and economic requirements of the local market. Some of these requirements include converting to the metric system, changing the size and shape of the package, and labeling. Aside from legally required changes, you may find that you have to tailor your product's flavor or fragrance to regional preferences. Canada Dry Co. makes 14 different flavors of orange soda for differing tastes throughout the world. Similarly, you may have to replace original product contents with local materials to please the host government, lower the price to please the consumer, or add protective packaging for hot, humid climates. (Quaker Oats uses vacuum tins in the tropics.) U.S. furniture makers have found that the large pieces of furniture that are the most popular in the United States cannot be sold in Japan, where apartments are tiny by U.S. standards.

Some product features are often inappropriate for particular regions. In some developing countries, dietetic features of foods such as no-salt or no-sugar products would be ridiculed. Consumers in those countries want their salt and sugar and don't want to be cheated out of valuable nutrients. Similarly, a bank that advertises free gifts if a customer brings in a new depositor may fail in a country where people never discuss personal finances with each other. In the developing world, usage instructions may have to be modified for less literate consumers. Pictures and movies are often used to instruct consumers in those countries.

Brand names are the subject of a long history of expensive bloopers. Everyone knows the hilarious error made by General Motors when it called its new model Nova and test-marketed it in Latin America: "No va" means "It doesn't go" in Spanish, and the car bombed spectacularly in Latin America until its name was changed to Caribe. Ford didn't fare much better with the Fiera, a truck targeted to the developing world. In certain Latin American countries the name "Fiera" means "ugly old woman." Citibank in Japan was often pronounced "She-tee-bank" until the problem was overcome by the choice of a written character used to pronounce the word correctly. In many cases, translations are not enough, and total rewriting may be necessary.

Sometimes the design of a product is unsuitable for a certain market, regardless of the packaging, advertising, and product name. There is a great market in the developing world for refrigerators, water pumps, and heavy farm equipment. In many of the rural areas, however, there is erratic or no electricity to drive these products. A company that would produce solar-powered refrigerators, windmill-driven water pumps, and pedal-powered farm equipment could make a fortune. Even in areas where there is electricity, many countries do not have skilled technicians to operate sophisticated equipment. A major way for you to win large sales and contracts for your company is to show the home office how less-sophisticated equipment could be sold profitably and how existing equipment could be modified. For example, a truck designed for U.S. highway use can be redesigned for the deserts of Africa or the rain forests of South America. Another way to sell sophisticated equipment in a less-developed country would be to offer to train mechanics and workers in the use of the products.

Success in many overseas markets means developing or modifying products to the needs of that market. Companies must employ the marketing concept rther than the sales concept. The sales concept states, "Here is the product, where can we sell it?" while the marketing concept states, "What does the consumer need and how can we produce it?"

A major error often made by U.S. marketers is treating Europe like part of the domestic market simply because it is part of the developed world. While a fairly high standard of living is enjoyed by most people throughout Europe, there are vast differences in the levels of development. The upper and middle classes show similar consumer behavior patterns throughout the Europen Community, but new entrants to the European Community such as Spain and Portugal still lag behind the northern countries in purchasing power.

Another error is treating all of Europe as if it were one country. There is no European consumer as such. Your overall marketing strategies for London would be somewhat different from those in the outlying areas of the United Kingdom and quite different from those aimed at the Portuguese farmer or Greek fisherman. Tastes differ widely throughout Europe, as the U.S. manufacturers of Tang orange drink found out. Orange juice and drink are preferred unsweetened in the U.K.; even the fresh orange juice served in Britain would be considered bitter by the U.S. consumer. When Tang was reformulated for the British palate, it sold well. The product had trouble in Germany too, but due to its name, not taste. When a German word was substituted, sales increased.

With the elimination of trade barriers between the countries of the European Community in 1992 (discussed in Chapter 6), many of the differences among European countries will decrease, but they will not disappear overnight. For example, microwave ovens, which are universal in the United States, are established only in some parts of Europe and very scarce in others; this will obviously affect the types of frozen foods that can be sold in Europe and how they are marketed. On the other hand, there will clearly be an opportunity for a single dominant pan-European brand to emerge in some areas such as financial services, computers, and retailing.

At the same time that Western Europe is consolidating, new opportunities are opening up in the Eastern bloc. As the Soviet Union and other Eastern European countries are liberalizing their economic policies, there will be increased opportunities to meet the great demand for Western consumer goods.

Europeans like products such as catsup, mustard, mayonnaise, and salad dressings in toothpaste-like tubes. This seems strange to Americans, but U.S. companies interested in selling dressings and condiments should repackage their products for mass market consumption in Europe. There are always specialty shops where glass jars of foods imported from the United States will sell because of the mystique or curiosity value of imports, but for the European lower and middle classes, it's dressing in tubes!

Nestle, the huge Swiss coffee maker, sells its products in every country in the non-Communist world, but makes different coffees for different countries based on taste preferences. The Nescafe in Switzerland tastes very different from the Nescafe in France. The advertising for these coffees is also keyed to local tastes. Other companies have found that they can sell the identical product in many different countries but must advertise it differently. Heineken beer is positioned as a premium import in the United States but as a proletarian beer in Great Britain.

Japan is a large consumer of U.S. goods, although to look at the imbalance of trade between Japan and the United States you wouldn't think so. Changing tastes and Westernization have opened up a vast consumer market in that country. McDonalds flourishes in Japan. Indeed, American products have such a cachet in Japan that many Japanese-made products are advertised in Japan with ads filmed in the United States. In Japan's crowded cities, ads depicting the wide open spaces of the American West have become extremely popular.

By the same token, the United States is a great consumer of Japanese goods. The Japanese have become the largest competitor of the United States, particularly in electronic equipment and other consumer products. In the 1950s and 1960s Japanese goods were considered a joke destined to fall apart as soon as you got them home. In less than 25 years Japanese goods have become synonymous with quality, and compete ferociously with the United States and Germany for markets in the developed and developing worlds.

While there is tremendous consumer demand for U.S. goods in

Japan, there are still tariff and nontariff barriers to sale of those goods. The United States continually threatens to (and occasionally does) impose quotas on Japanese goods, and Japan continually promises to open up its markets. But for companies that persevere, the Japanese market is a most lucrative one. U.S. firms can and do succeed in Japan, despite barriers to entry.

Many countries in the developing world, particularly in Latin America, want U.S. goods and services. Most recently, however, the strength of the dollar has made it prohibitive for them to buy from the United States. Harsh financing and credit terms and demand for payment in dollars often result in Latin Americans purchasing goods from Europe, Japan, or one of the Southeast Asian newcomers. Taiwan, Singapore, South Korea, and Hong Kong have become aggressive competitors and are producing high-quality goods at low prices. Let's not forget the way Japan penetrated the Latin American telecommunications market in the 1960s. Although the Latin Americans were ostensibly satisfied with the U.S. products they had been purchasing, they switched to Japanese suppliers because Japan sold products that were comparable to (or only slightly below) the U.S. goods in quality and at more reasonable prices. Low price, combined with a distinct ability to "massage" the purchasing executives, brought about strong sales for the Japanese. They unquestionably understood their products and their markets.

Consumer and industrial markets are continually changing and expanding. While the U.S., European, and Japanese youth populations are declining, the developing world has a huge youth market potential. In addition, the "gray" market of older, affluent consumers in Europe and Japan is a thriving one. Adapt, modify, package, promote, and then go out and make a deal!

13

Your Power Presence

"Being a foreigner is so weird to the Japanese, that the marginal impact of being a woman is nothing," says a female personnel vice president of Bank of America's Asia Division. While being a foreigner is not nearly as unusual in some of the less homogeneous societies of other Asian, European, and Latin American countries, being a U.S. businesswoman in these places will almost always capture everyone's attention. Nonetheless, the reaction is very often positive. As a businesswoman you are seen much more as a "foreign executive" who happens to be a woman than as a "woman" who has a more traditional role in the local society. Especially in developing countries, the fact that you look different from the locals helps your clients to see you as "executive" rather than "woman."

For example, on hearing that I was waiting for my scheduled meeting in the reception area, one of the Brazilian Central bankers I was to meet asked his secretary in Portuguese, "Did you say Mister Rossman is a woman?" He had not, in our earlier correspondences by telex and mail, realized that I was a woman. Understanding enough Portuguese to realize his surprise, my gut knotted at the prospect of dealing with what I assumed to be strong prejudice. When he emerged to greet me a minute later, I was prepared to be defensive, and stood stiffly while shaking hands. To my surprise, he was warm and friendly, and told me that it hadn't occurred to him that I was a woman. He had assumed (correctly) that anyone he was dealing with had to be on a high level, and (incorrectly) would therefore be a man. In order to allow him to save face, I did not point out that my name could hardly be mistaken for a man's (though it often is—I routinely get mail from overseas addressed to me as "Mister"). I did mention that I had come up with a new idea to generate Brazilian export credits. His interest and excitement over my suggestion was so strong that, after formalities and coffees, we worked for four hours. He never mentioned the fact of my being a woman again.

The Brazilian banker's surprise at finding I was a woman was by no means an isolated incident. Nevertheless, after the shock wore off, my clients at other Latin American meetings were, for the most part, amenable to doing business with me. My knowledge of and experience in each country had much to do with my being accepted. The best way to overcome initial resistance is to show your expertise at the first appropriate occasion. You want to be judged on your ability and skill, not on the basis of gender.

When you enter a meeting room, stand tall even if you're only five feet high. Your height is unimportant; it's your posture that gives clues about your expertise and your general feeling toward yourself. If you're in a high-stress situation and don't know exactly where to put your hands, try the power move popularized by the British royal family: Stand tall, with one palm gripping the other hand behind the back. You'll look confident, authoritative, and even regal! The first impression will tell your client either that you are in control and self-confident or that you are anxious and unsure. If you don't feel confident, fake it. Shake hands firmly or bow as the formalities dictate. If you have been delayed and arrive late, don't rush in apologizing while gasping for air. Arriving late in many countries is appropriate. When late in Europe, simply compose yourself and apologize briefly.

While it is important to behave, dress, and carry yourself like the executive you are, it is not necessary to present yourself as a gray-flannel neuter. What does the businesswoman wear to set off her powerful presence? Never a floppy bow tie! A totally "male" dress style is never appropriate. Beyond this one generality, clothes should vary with the temperature and personality of the place. For example, in Rio de Janeiro, Brazil, a good cotton, silk, or linen-blend dress is appropriate. In São Paulo, an hour away from Rio by air, a light grey, taupe, peach, or other soft-colored suit is your best bet. In the tropical and informal bikinied atmosphere of Rio, a suit is not only uncomfortable but also stuffy looking. In the more temperate, business-oriented climate of São Paulo, a suit is appropriate, but a dark suit is too somber for the Brazilian personality.

You can wear your navy blue suit in places that have a cold climate, stress conformity and formality, or have a strong U.S. orientation. In many parts of Europe, your navy blue suit and a colorful soft blouse are excellent choices. Because of strong animal-rights attitudes in many parts of Europe, it is not a good idea to wear a fur coat there. Save the fur for the northern United States and buy a good-quality cloth coat. You'll worry less about loss or theft, and no one will ever spray paint your loden coat. Your grey or navy suit worn with a good blouse is the proper uniform for Japan, too. Avoid slacks and heavily starched, man-tailored blouses. You can wear dresses in most places if you are more comfortable in them. Take a blazer along if you want a jacket for warmth or for a more powerful look. Well-cut silk, wool, or cotton dresses are appropriate anywhere.

Save sandals, heavy makeup, long, glamorous hair, strong perfume, sheer blouses, heavy jewelry, and large purses for a nonbusiness event. You do not want your clients to be distracted from your purpose, which is negotiating and closing the deal. You want to look attractive, not seductive or unprofessional.

Recent studies at Yale, New York University, and other universities have shown that being attractive has negative consequences for executive women. However, being attractive is considered an advantage for men. Some researchers have gone so far as to say that women should try to appear as unattractive and masculine as possible if they want to succeed in their careers. More moderate researchers have suggested that very attractive women should seek to play down their attractiveness if they want to be judged on their ability.

Nonetheless, don't worry about playing down your femininity with your overseas client—you are not competing with him, nor are you his wife, date, daughter, or friend. You can look attractive as long as your bearing shouts "professional." There is nothing that states that purpose better than a solid-color, well-cut, below-the-knee suit, skirt, or dress; mid-high-heeled pumps; neutral panty hose; and a gentle but firm handshake. Recently, shoe manufacturers in the United States have brought out low-heeled pumps that are stylish yet well-cushioned for long hours of walking and standing.

If you have very long hair, pull it away from your face in a french twist or knot. You don't have to look unfeminine, just businesslike. Short to medium-length hair should also be combed away from the face. Avoid colorful barrettes and dangling earrings. One good piece of jewelry, like a pin or a strand of pearls, is in good taste.

I usually do not carry a briefcase on overseas trips, although I always carry one in the United States. If I don't need to go over my papers on the plane trip, I put them in a "Redweld" legal-size, expandable cardboard folder, and pack them in my carry-on bag. Although I don't carry a purse with my briefcase at home, I carry a good leather shoulder-strap purse overseas. But if you need your briefcase on your trip, don't carry a purse too. Put a small clutch purse into your briefcase for your personal items, and carry it on board the plane. You don't want to arrive at a meeting overburdened. Picture yourself fumbling with a heavy briefcase, an umbrella, a purse, address directions, and possibly a map. I like the shoulder purse and Redweld combination because I can tuck the folder under my arm and have both my hands free. Also, with the Redweld packed, I have one less piece of luggage to worry about.

Of course, to find out the best way to put yourself together, observe the locals. The problem with this tactic is that you have to pack before you get there. The next best thing is to find out about the climate of the place along with the degree of traditionalism. In the Middle East—for example, if you are working in Saudi Arabia—be prepared to take calf-length midi skirts and long-sleeved loose-fitting blouses along. Or you could purchase the loose-flowing ankle-length dress that Arab women wear. You do not need to wear a veil under any circumstances, but you may be more comfortable in the fashionble long dress that has been called "Koran chic" in honor of the revival of the fundamentalist dictates of the Islamic religion. In less conservative places like Egypt, Jordan, Bahrain, and the United Arab Emirates, a woman can comfortably wear a plain suit or long-sleeved dress. Of course, in Israel a woman can wear whatever she wishes, although a light-colored, loose cotton garment is most comfortable for the climate.

Although most synthetic fabrics don't wrinkle, they retain body heat and often look cheap. A blend of 65 percent linen and 35 percent polyester, however, looks beautiful, doesn't wrinkle much, and breathes. I usually travel with a few silk/cotton-blend blouses that can be washed in a hotel sink and hung up to dry on a padded hanger. These blouses need little or no ironing if you hang them to dry carefully. After a number of bad experiences dry-cleaning my silk blouses in Latin America, I now try to avoid having my clothes cleaned anywhere in the world. The silk/cotton blend blouses are reasonably priced, luxurious, and hand-washable. Best of all, you can keep your anxiety level down by rinsing them out with your pantyhose.

Wherever you travel, and no matter what blouses or dresses you wear, be sure they cover the entire neck area. The "neck dimple" is a vulnerable area and a subliminal sign of invitation—not necessarily a sexual invitation as much as a sign of harmlessness and lack of power. If need be, drape a scarf around your neck.

So now you are beautifully dressed, poised, and confident, and the negotiations have gone well. What about taking your client to lunch or dinner? You hesitate. So much has been written on power lunching in the United States (who picks up the check, where to go, and what to drink) that it seems like an insurmountable task, even compared to the exhausting negotiating you've just been through. In fact, it's probably easier to accomplish a power lunch with your overseas client than at home, where you might lose points for eating sushi or quiche. If you have the opportunity before you go, read up on the food of the country. Don't hesitate to ask someone for a restaurant recommendation or have your client pick out a favorite restaurant and make a reservation. Don't worry about your power presence at lunch or dinner, as you've already shown your authority and ability at the meeting. The United States is one of the few countries in the world where business deals are made over a meal. In most other countries, lunch or dinner is a place to relax a bit and enjoy. So don't continue discussing the business deal once you arrive at the restaurant. Knowledge of music, art, and literature is highly respected in most countries. Your college liberal-arts courses will come in handy here.

One of the most useful things you can do during lunch is to draw your client out and learn about him and his country. One way to begin is to ask about his family. Everywhere in the world except Saudi Arabia and other very traditional Arab countries, questions about family are welcomed. While it is unlikely that you will be asked to dine with a Saudi Arabian client, if you do, keep the conversation to the climate and the technological advances of the country.

Avoid trying to look into a Saudi's eyes. In the United States, someone who doesn't look you in the eye seems suspicious, but in Saudi Arabia and other very traditional Arab countries it may be considered hostile or, worse, intimate. In Japan it is considered rude to look someone deeply in the eyes. Try to be conscious of this habit. Arabs often wear dark glasses so you won't be able to see the changes in their pupils, which give away vital information. Outside Western Europe and Latin America, try to gaze less directly at your client.

If your client asks you about your family, tell him briefly. Before I was married, I routinely invented a fiancé to forestall comments about what a shame it was that I was alone. By skillfully asking your client about his family you can learn a great deal. Avoid giving out a lot of information about yourself, however.

Another topic of conversation is the client's country. Tell him, for instance, that you are interested in a specific city, and he will probably give you a short travelogue. Think of how informed you'll sound for your next client when you discuss the virtues of San Flores. Even if you only have time to skim a travel guide to your client's country, pick out something in which you are genuinely interested and ask your client to tell you about it. Your client will think you a well-informed and intelligent individual. People all over the world love to talk about their favorite subject, themselves. Given the opportunity, they will respond informatively to questions such as "What music and arts do your enjoy?" or "What parts of your country do you like best?" Avoid controversial subjects like the status of local women in business, if you want a pleasant meal.

If your client urges you to talk about yourself, give anecdotes about the United States in general and your city in particular. My clients love to hear about apartment prices in New York, and about the city's dangers, cultural activities, and incredibly fast pace. No matter where you live, stories about the United States fascinate people from all over the world. If you can laugh at some of the idiosyncracies of the United States, you will feel at ease and will also put your client at ease. Then you can settle down to the real business at hand, enjoying your meal.

While you may have read guidelines against ordering certain foods at a power lunch lest your prestige be diminished, there is a growing movement in the United States for even the most macho of business executives to eat lightly. I had lunch in New York recently with the head of worldwide marketing of one of the largest financial services companies in the United States. He ordered a turkey sandwich, coleslaw, mineral water, and fresh fruit for dessert. Hardly the stuff of power lunching, right? Wrong! The trend toward fitness and coronary health has led many men away from heavy, rich food. There is a growing movement among U.S. executives to live long enough to enjoy their six-figure incomes.

Most high-power executives overseas are not eating turkey sandwiches and coleslaw for lunch, however, and neither would you. For one thing, you would probably have to go to the American Club or a U.S.-style restaurant for it, and unless you are certain your client likes U.S.-style food, you are better off having lunch on your client's turf. Remember, a meal overseas is not a struggle for supremacy, just pure enjoyment, and part of the enjoyment of travel is trying the local cuisine.

One rule of thumb is that when inland, avoid ordering seafood, especially in the developing world. Broiled meats and chicken are excellent choices. If you are in a coastal area anywhere in the world, you will probably enjoy the seafood most. But avoid raw shellfish everywhere in the developing world. In most of South America, beef is prized. It is grass-fed rather than grain-fed, and cut differently than in the United States. If you have never tasted steak like the kind served in Buenos Aires, Argentina, or São Paulo, Brazil, you are in for a treat. It is less fatty than U.S. beef, and sweeter.

In Japan, the beef is also special, and you can order steaks shabu shabu and sukiyaki. In the rest of Asia, take advantage of the superb regional cuisine. Taste Chinese food that is nothing like your corner Cantonese restaurant. Here is your opportunity to have real Thai food, Indonesian rijstaffel, Malaysian satays, and Indian curries.

By all means, order mineral water. It was drunk by everyone, everywhere in the world, long before U.S. yuppies discovered Perrier. Since tap water may be less than relible outside the United States, everyone drinks bottled water with meals.

Even if you don't enjoy drinking, order something alcoholic, if only to toast your client and his country. You don't have to drink much or finish the glass, but it is part of the social ritual.

Although I enjoy a drink before dinner or wine with dinner, I find it difficult to drink during lunch. Probably due to the fact that I equate having a drink with my leisure time, I can't return to work after lunch-hour drinking. In the United States I simply don't order alcohol. When I am overseas, however, I always order beer or a glass of wine during lunch, even if I don't drink much of it. Once, during some particularly sticky negotiations in the Dominican Republic, I invited my client to lunch. Knowing that in that country, as in all the Caribbean, drinking expensive imported Scotch is a status symbol even though the local rum is superb, I ordered Scotch whiskey. My client, a self-important macho type and a somewhat difficult individual, was surprised and blurted out, "But that's a real man's drink!" I replied that I loved the aroma and taste of good Scotch. (As it hapens, I do, although not at lunch.) He was so impressed that he didn't even notice how little of it I drank. Although situations like this are exceptions, the usual rule of thumb is to order whatever beverage the country is famous for. The beer is superb in Germany, Holland, and most of the developing world. Wine is magnificent in Italy, France, Spain, Chile, and Argentina. Whiskeys are excellent in the United Kingdom. When I am in Puerto Rico on business, my favorite after-dinner drink is a little-known aged, dark rum that is exported in small quantities. It is a rich, cognac-like spirit produced in small batches by Ron Barrilito. I doubt that I have won any contracts by ordering it, but the fact that I know of it certainly does impress my clients.

At the end of your meal, when you and your client both reach for the check say, "Please allow me the honor of buying you lunch [or dinner]." If he puts up a fight or argues loudly, allow him to pick up the check and ask for a return engagement at which you can buy him a meal. If your language ability is excellent, or if the management speaks English, politely ask the captain to give you the check. This should be done during a trip to the telephone or washroom. Whatever happens, don't try to explain that you are on an expense account, and don't argue with your client about the check. That's where a real loss of power can occur. If you feel uncomfortable about not paying for the meal, or fear he will not allow you to pick up the check, send him a small impersonal gift, like a small appliance, book, or ashtray, along with your business card and a thank you note.

Aside from lunch, dinner, or a drink, you may not enjoy socializing with your overseas clients. There are some exceptions, however, when socializing is part of the business ritual. In Japan, it is quite common for people to go out and drink in the evening. If you feel this ritual is part of the requirement of doing business, by all means participate in it. Eat beforehand and match toasts but try to drink as little as possible. At best you'll be hung over, and at worst your tongue will loosen so that you will regret what you said, even if you don't give out any industrial secrets. But in Japan it is considered bad form to repeat or use to advantage what others have said while under the influence of alcohol. When others are drinking, they rarely count how many you've had, so go in the spirit of friendship, but go easy with the spirits.

Part of establishing your power presence includes knowing little things about the country in which you're dealing. You gain a tremendous advantage by surprising your client with things that he thinks are known only within the boundaries of his country. Knowing a phrase in the language, a dish that is famous, or a part of the country that is regarded with pride are some of the things that can make you stand out from the competition. While you do not want to try to become a compatriot (you would lose your mystique and advantage) you must learn as much as you can about the culture, and play by their rules.

As a woman you have a tremendous advantage: You are an unknown quantity. One of my clients in Milan, Italy, lit up like a Christmas tree when he saw that M. Rossman was a woman and spoke some

Italian. He said he was expecting a tall man in a baggy suit and heavy oxfords who couldn't pronounce his name, wore a college ring, and shook his hand so hard that the crest of the ring imprinted on his finger. Since it was the first time he had dealt professionally with a businesswoman from the United States, he seemed a little uncertain about how to treat me. The attitudes and rules that he went by when doing business with a U.S. businessman obviously didn't seem right to him, nor did he seem inclined to behave toward me the way Italian men behave toward Italian women. I could sense his confusion. I didn't rush to open the door for myself or insist that he did not stand up when I came into a room, and most of all I didn't scold him when he told me that "it was a pleasure to do business with an attractive lady." All these things, which would have irritated me in the United States, seemed somehow natural in Italy. I couldn't afford to become sidetracked by little irritations. The guidelines that we all follow in the United States aren't valid overseas. Use this to your advantage, take the lead, and make up the rules for yourself and your client—that's real power!

14

Life on the Road: Traveling for Business

There is a tremendous mystique surrounding an overseas trip, even when (and often especially when) it's for business. Your friends are envious, your husband or partner is jealous, your parents are nervous (what will my little girl do all alone in Hong Kong?) while you are making exciting arrangements for your meetings. Rewarding? Yes! But glamorous? No! Think of the "glamour" of stumbling off a plane, jet-lagged, having been bored to tears by a garrulous seatmate during your 14-hour flight, and having to go to a meeting in 2 hours. Even more "glamorous" is trying to negotiate a deal with a dyed-in-the-wool believer in keeping women barefoot and pregnant, who is offering you endless cups of coffee while you're suffering from a case of *turista*.

Certainly, business travel can be glamorous at times, although there are ways to minimize the discomforts. But even at the worst moments, remember that you are doing this for the future of your career, so pack your eye drops and Lomotil, follow the jet lag diet, peel your vegetables—and knock 'em dead!

If you are exhausted, suffering from stomach problems, or just plain disoriented, don't let on, as it may have a bad impact on your dealings. When Secretary of State George Schultz met with Soviet president Andrei Gromyko a while back, Mr. Gromyko asked casually if Mr. Schultz was travel-weary. Mr. Schultz, wisely realizing that revealing a weakness could disadvantage his negotiations, said he had slept on the plane. Whether or not he had slept is unimportant. What mattered is that he did not reveal any information that could have been used against him.

You can do many things to counteract jet lag, illness, and lack of sleep. If you are traveling to Europe or South America and have the luxury of a day flight, take advantage of it. You can go to sleep when you arrive and be fresh for the next day's business. When booking your flight, be aware of the fact that on most airlines, you can get your boarding pass, or at least a seat assignment, up to 30 days before you fly. If you travel business or first class there are lounges to wait in before the flight. If you are a frequent flyer you can often use bonus points to upgrade your seat to first class. All this is designed to cut down on the standing on line, rushing, and crowding in the airport that can increase your exhaustion. Because of the long time needed to fly to the Far East, along with the added disorientation that comes from crossing the international date line, you should allow yourself a full day to adjust, if possible. Many corporations are becoming aware of the importance of adjusting your circadian rhythms (body clock) to the locale. They encourage executives flying long distances to change their diets and schedules to maximize success in negotiating.

Many experienced travelers swear by the jet lag diet, a four-day regimen of controlled eating and drinking that is aimed at helping your body adjust to changes in time zones. The details of this diet have been reported in the travel sections of many newspapers and magazines. If you are the type who suffers badly from jet lag, or if you are taking a flight that will carry you across many time zones (such as flying from New York to Tokyo, a difference of 14 hours), you might want to investigate this diet.

If this diet seems too much trouble to follow, or if you don't have four days in which to follow it (for example, if you are given an emergency assignment and your meeting is the next day), you can still minimize the effect of jet lag. The most important thing is to avoid caffeine and alcohol on the flight. While it's tempting to drink coffee, cocktails, or both on the plane, alcohol and caffeine are the two substances that cause the worst symptoms of jet lag. Your body is prone to dehydration in the desert-dry atmosphere of an airplane, and caffeine and alcohol compound the problem. Drink lots of juices and water. Eat lightly and try to nap. You can order special meals on most airlines at no extra cost. If available, try the fruit plate or the vegetarian meal. Besides being lighter and healthier, they are, in many cases, the best-tasting food you can order. Another good bet is the low-sodium dinner, which also helps to fight dehydration because it lacks the excessive salt common to typical airline food. Low-sodium, fruit, and vegetarian meals also usually come with fresh fruit instead of the desiccated, overly sweet desserts that the regular airline meals feature.

Try to sleep on the plane, or at least close your eyes and rest. Picture what people are doing at your destination and set your watch to that time. Buy a sleep mask and use it. If nothing else, it may help to discourage seatmates who are anxious to talk. If your flight isn't full, find a row of empty seats, get some pillows and a blanket, and stretch out. On a flight to Peru that was interrupted by a landing in Miami for minor repairs, I dozed for an hour in a row of seats, and read and rested the remainder of the trip. Although I was on the plane for over 14 hours, I felt relatively refreshed when I arrived. If you have an interesting seatmate and wish to talk, do so, but not for the entire flight. You'll most likely be staying in the same city, so you can meet the next day if you want.

If you haven't had the chance to read extensively about the country in which you'll be working, this is the time. Take along a paperback that deals with the culture of the country. Try to avoid business reading at this time, if you can. If you're looking for a little escape reading, a spy or romantic novel might be just the thing: if it's a well-written novel, it will help to pass the time; if it's bad it may help you fall asleep! Sometimes you may have to work during your flight. Begin the work as soon as you get on the plane. When you finish you can relax, nap, or read a novel.

Packing a few extra paperbacks is a good idea, especially if you are traveling to Southeast Asia, the Middle East, or Latin America. You may find the selection in hotel shops limited to two-year-old titles at steep prices. English-language paperbacks are easier to find in most of Europe. Discarding the paperbacks after you've read them lightens your luggage for the return flight, leaving precious space for the gifts you'll be bringing home. You may also want to pack a Walkman and music or language tapes.

Try to pack as little as possible. If you are going on a trip for a short time, take travel sizes of all cosmetics, medications, and appliances. Pack cosmetics in unbreakable plastic containers. I keep a kit packed with all the shampoo, creams, aspirins, toothpaste, and dental floss I need for up to three weeks on the road. It's wonderful for fast and frequent getaways.

Some other travel aids you may want are a mini hair dryer with dual voltage, a set of international electric plugs and/or adapters, a tiny first aid kit, a sewing kit, a Swiss army knife, a travel iron, a portable alarm clock, a flash-light and matches, an umbrella, plastic bags, a pocket calculator, packets of Woolite, a camera and film, tampons, and any necessary prescription drugs. You can get all these items in small sizes or quantities. For those traveling in somewhat dangerous areas, or for the very cautious, there are portable door alarms, portable door jambs, and deadbolts, which can be mail-ordered or purchased from sporting goods and specialty shops in the United States.

Change a few dollars at a foreign exchange bank at home. Sometimes airport banks are crowded or closed when you arrive. Have enough foreign currency with you when you land to tip the airport porter and pay for a cab to your hotel.

Keep all your documents and medications, a few cosmetics, and your toothbrush in your carry-on luggage. If your baggage is lost, it's comforting to know you can argue with the airline officials with clean teeth, and with your medications, cash, and papers tucked into your tote bag. You can then meet with your client, secure in the knowledge that the airline is doing everything possible to find your bags, and still have clean teeth and fresh lipstick. For the same reason, the directions to the meeting should be carried with you, as should at least the most essential of your business documents.

Packing everything in a garment bag is the best way to cut down on the possibility of lost baggage and to get to your hotel without waiting for what seems like hours at the baggage carousel. These bags hold an enormous amount of clothing and can be carried onto the plane and hung up in the on-board coat closet.

If you are going to wear suits to your meetings and are staying for up to three weeks, two suits and a contrasting skirt are all you need. The suit jackets can serve as blazers for the extra skirt. Take tailored blouses for the daytime and dressy ones for evenings. A strapless camisole top made out of silk or linen with a softly tailored suit makes a superb evening outfit. If you have to entertain clients, keep the jacket on; if you are dating or going to a nonbusiness function, you can take it off. Add a dress, some interesting accessories, sports clothing appropriate to the climate and culture of the country, and comfortable shoes. All this can be packed into a garment bag. Your other necessities go into a carry-on shoulder tote which also usually holds a tremendous amount. Don't bother with a purse for the trip—you need your hands free to maneuver. If you must have a purse, you can pack a small one in the garment bag. If you are wearing dresses, take three or four good ones whose looks can be changed by adding a blazer, costume jewelry, a belt, and a silk scarf.

Whatever you're wearing, don't overpack. You may want to shop a little during your free time. Western Europe is a particularly good place for U.S. women to buy clothing and accessories. The clothing is often cut to fit us without alterations. In the Far East and Latin America, the cut is somewhat less suited to American women, but here too you can buy some good clothing and plenty of beautiful accessories.

No matter where you are, though, you may find an unexpected bargain. On one of my business trips to Rio, I spent my entire free day shopping in the fancy Ipanema boutiques featuring $250 designer dresses, but couldn't find anything that fit me properly. A few days later, I had two hours to kill between meetings, and I wandered into a nearby shopping center. In a very unpretentious women's clothing store, I found a beautiful black cocktail dress hanging on a pipe rack and bearing a $30 price tag. It needed only a few alterations to fit me perfectly. The dress always gets compliments when I wear it at New York parties, and I always reply, "That? That's just a little number I picked up in Rio."

Try to have some input into which hotels you'll be staying in, if your company or its travel agent allows. I always try to pick a hotel owned by a U.S., Canadian, or major international chain. Staying in a small, quaint hotel may be very pleasant in London or Paris, but in the smaller cities of Europe or in the developing world, you should stick with a large, international establishment. Though often cold and impersonal, these large chains are more used to seeing businesswomen, and often offer telexes, photocopying, safe deposit boxes, valets, and other business and personal services. Large hotel chains frequently have swimming pools, saunas, and exercise rooms as well. Many large hotels can get you a guest pass to a tennis or golf club if you request it. Keep in shape by exercising in your room if your hotel doesn't have any sports or exercise facilities. A businesswoman friend of mine travels with a jump rope and works out with it daily.

If your hotel doesn't provide business and other services, ask the concierge to help you. In most major cities in the world you can get secretarial services, translators, conference rooms, and audiovisual equipment. Particularly in the developing world, a small, discreet tip to the concierge makes these things happen as if by magic.

Large hotels often have good restaurants and comfortable lounges. I've eaten dinner alone in many high-quality rooftop hotel restaurants around the world. Hotel coffee shops usually offer substantial meals if you want comfort and informality.

You don't have to limit yourself to your hotel, however, unless you're in a small town in the developing world or in parts of the Middle East. Elsewhere, when you have the time, try the best local restaurants. Ask for a list of good restaurants or look them up in a travel guide, and take yourself to one. Dining alone can be one of the most pleasant aspects of a business trip. Make a reservation at the restaurant, order wine, and sit back and reflect on how well you've done. A woman friend who never goes to good restaurants alone in New York, where she lives, goes to dinner alone in most of the places to which she travels. She feels less out of place dining alone overseas than she does at home.

When you are dining alone you can explore different restaurants. Take your clients to the international establishments—you don't want any surprises. But an unusual dish or drink in a restaurant halfway around the world can be a rare pleasure to be savored when you're dining alone.

A few years ago, during a particularly stressful round of meetings in Venezuela, I found myself with a completely free weekend. I was staying in Caracas at a large U.S.-owned hotel that had full services and a pool. Saturday I swam, had an excellent massage, had my hair shampooed in the beauty salon, and ordered an excellent dinner and wine from room service. Sunday I repeated the procedure and went to dinner at a nearby restaurant. By Monday morning I was refreshed and ready to continue my battles. I was able to win the contract for my company, a fact that I partially attribute to my relaxing weekend.

A woman acquaintance spends her free time on business trips dieting. During the evenings that she has dinner with her clients she eats regular meals, but when she is on her own she often goes to a green grocer and brings an assortment of fresh fruit and vegetables back to her room. If you want to try this, travel with a can opener, knife, fork, spoon, and cork screw.

When you are on the road for a long period of time, it's a good idea to pamper yourself. Do things that you wouldn't do ordinarily. Although I have never ridden in a hansom cab around Central Park in New York, I rode in one during a stay in Guadalajara, Mexico. It was a lovely ride, marred only by the driver's insistence that he would pick me up later that night in his hansom cab.

As a woman traveling alone, you may be harassed by that particular assortment of weirdos that are permanent fixtures in every country. Rude or patronizing clerks, porters, waiters, managers, and so forth can be found all over the world. Many hotels in the U.S. have recently introduced special seminars for instructing their personnel on correct behavior toward female guests. Unfortunately, this is not yet the case in most of the world. At any rate, unpleasant experiences can still happen to you when you're traveling alone, whether you're in New York, St. Louis, Rome, or Hong Kong. (Men, too, are sometimes treated rudely.) Don't hesitate to complain to the management if you are not being treated properly.

When you check in, be conscious of those around you. Take the key and ask for a bellboy. This way you can be sure that the room is ready, and can have the bellboy explain where the electrical outlets and extra blankets are if you need them.

Use caution when depositing and picking up your key. There is no more irritating situation than to receive a phone call from some inebriated character who saw your room number hours earlier when you were picking up your key. All hotels have a security staff. Don't hesitate to use them if you have to.

If you are traveling to a city or region that has had any incidence of kidnapping, terrorism, or mugging, use extra caution on the streets and in the hotel. In this case a portable door alarm or door jamb might make sense. Be certain to use only licensed and metered cabs. In most places, however, your usual common sense is enough protection.

Getting sick on your trip during an important series of meetings can be devastating. There is no guarantee against illness, but you can cut down on your chances of becoming seriously ill. Many people experience mild discomfort when they travel anywhere, even to another state in the United States, due to the changes in water, climate, and altitude. It's normal then to expect some changes when traveling thousands of miles. Some places in the developing world do not have the same sanitary standards as London or Paris, but you can get sick anywhere in the world, even at home. One of the worst cases of intestinal illness I've ever had happened after I ate tainted shellfish in New York.

Check with the Center for Disease Control in Atlanta or the World

Health Hotline in your city before you leave. If immunization shots are recommended, take them. The protection is worth the small amount of discomfort. Be especially careful of food and drink in the developing world. Always drink *carbonated* bottled water, because an unscrupulous waiter could fill a bottle with tap water and present it to you as just opened. If you are unsure about the ice cubes, drink your cocktails mixed with chilled juice or soda, or better yet, drink beer, which is safe everywhere.

As a general rule, don't eat uncooked fruit, vegetetables, or fish in the developing world. Avoid shellfish, custard fillings, creams, and cheeses unless you are sure that they have been properly refrigerated and prepared. Your best bets in the developing world are cooked meats and poultry, soups and stews, rice, potatoes, and cooked greens.

If, even after using extreme caution, you become ill, try to avoid self-medicating. Routine traveler's diarrhea, which is painless, mild, and lasts from one to three days, is very different from the severe, painful diarrhea that can indicate a more serious illness. Eat very lightly and avoid dehydration by drinking canned or bottled fruit juice. Soup, tea, bread and crackers, colas, rice, and bananas are recommended. If you must attend an important meeting, Lomotil or Kaopectate will lessen the diarrheic episodes temporarily but they don't get rid of the disease. Recently, Immodium, an effective antidiarrheic formerly available only by prescritpion, has become available over-the-counter. Pepto Bismol, available almost everywhere, is effective as well. These medications should be used only for emergency situations. An English-speaking doctor in Mexico City once told me that taking these drugs is dangerous because your body can reabsorb the infection. The best thing, he felt, was to let severe diarrhea run its course, while taking antibiotics to prevent infecting the organs.

No matter what the symptoms, if you don't feel well after a day or two, call a doctor. It's a good idea to let the doctor know what medications you are allergic to, if you are traking oral contraceptives, or if you have any preexisting medical problems.

Large hotels often have a competent doctor on the staff. There are a number of organizations in the United States that will provide you with a list of English-speaking doctors throughout the world. Try the International Association for Medical Assistance to Travellers (IAMAT) or INTERMEDIC in New York. Medical insurance is available for travelers as well, so check with your insurer.

Unfortunately, malaria has not been eradicated in some parts of the developing world, and other mosquito-borne illnesses are still prevalent in some countries. If you're traveling to one of these countries, make sure you pack a can of mosquito repellent and, if you have any doubts, ask for a mosquito net at your hotel.

Don't be alarmed if your menstrual period arrives early or late. Flying often upsets the menstrual cycle slightly. Unless you are traveling to Western Europe, Japan, Hong Kong, or another major world capital, take along a supply of tampons if you use them. Sanitary napkins are easy to find throughout the world, but tampons are not always easily available in many places. If you anticipate having your menstrual period while traveling, it is comforting to have a supply of tampons in your suitcase.

The same goes for birth control pills, although sometimes they can be obtained in some surprising places. A woman who was traveling in rural Mexico had to stay longer than she anticipated and needed her next month's supply of birth control pills. Worried that as an unmarried American woman she would have a hard time obtaining a supply of pills in a strongly Catholic country, she went to a doctor's office armed with a long sob story about losing her pills and her husband not wanting any more children. Before she got to see the doctor, she tearfully explained her problem in broken Spanish to the receptionist, who told her to go next door to the pharmacy to buy the pills. When the woman explained that she didn't have her prescription with her, the receptionist said, "Just go next door and ask for Ovral." She did, and got the pills without a prescription. When she got them back to her hotel room she read the package and saw that they were manufactured in New Jersey! Nonetheless, some women have had a hard time getting contraceptives in foreign countries, so it's always a good idea to bring along whatever you think you'll need and maybe a little extra. Nowadays, condoms are widely available.

So, you've prepared for your trip, you've kissed friends, family, and lovers good-bye, and you're speeding to your destination. Then what? You certainly have your work and meetings cut out for you, but what will you do on the weekends and evenings when you don't have to work? For the first few days of work, just having dinner will be an effort, but as you adjust to the environment you will want to see people and sights, especially if you're lucky enough to be working in a great capital city. Certainly in places like London, Munich, Cairo, Hong Kong, and São Paulo, you will have no difficulty finding interesting things to do. Even in the smaller "second cities" there will be plenty of culture to absorb. If you are working in a small town, take a plane to the capital or to the nearest beach resort for the weekend and enjoy. Or simply stay in town and use this time to catch up on sleep. This is a good opportunity to soak in a tub, have a facial or massage, and read a good book. Small towns can be delightful too, and taking a tour or meeting the people can be a good way to spend your time.

Depending on the culture, spending your nonworking time may sometimes be a little more difficult than your working time. Your intelligence and professionalism has convinced your clients that a woman executive can be as good as or better than a man, but out of the business context, how are women alone regarded and treated? In most places today, especially in big cities, women alone are accepted, but in some places you may be seen as fair game. Men overseas have gotten used to seeing women tourists alone; but don't be surprised if you are approached by them. Twenty years ago a lone U.S. or British tourist to Spain would have an American flag or Union Jack propped up at her restaurant table to signal the locals that she wasn't a prostitute. Today, you can have lunch or dinner at many formerly all-male preserves without raising an eyebrow.

Socializing in most of Western Europe is somewhat similar to socializing in the United States. Of course, men will try to flirt with you, but that's nothing new. Latin America is quite a bit behind Western Europe, but certainly large cities like Buenos Aires, Rio de Janeiro, São Paulo, Lima, Caracas, Bogotá, and Mexico City are fairly comfortable for women travelers. In most of the big cities of the Far East, you can move about with relative ease, except in China and Japan. Activities are carefully monitored in China; and in Japan you'll probably spend a lot of time socializing with your clients, as business is pleasure there. You won't be able to move around unrestrictedly in much of the Middle East except for Egypt and Israel, but in the Gulf States you will be able to spend quality time with fascinating women.

An excellent way for single and married women to meet people is to spend time with a local family. Although I'm not religious, I have been using *The Jewish Travel Guide*, edited by Sidney Lightman (and published in the United Kingdom) for over ten years. When I was single and traveling to a new place, I'd write or call one of the congregations listed in this book. I would explain (sometimes in English, sometimes in the language of the country) that I was a young woman traveling on business, and that I wanted to meet a local family. To my great delight I almost always received warm and gracious hospitality. For example, I was picked up at the airport in Bogotá by a limousine whose chauffeur insisted that I come to the home of the family I had contacted by letter; I was invited to a large formal dinner in Mexico City; and I was introduced to an eligible dentist nephew in São Paulo. These people were as anxious to meet a U.S. woman as I was to meet a local family. While I don't know of any similar publications for other religions, the same effect may be accomplished by contacting the main church headquarters in your home city and asking for a listing of churches in any city overseas. If you're not a church member, try making overseas contacts through your athletic group, chess club, or other association. Since I've been married, I still use the same method, only now I refuse dates from eligible young dentists!

Another excellent way to meet people is through professional or university affiliations. I am an alumna of New York University (NYU) and belong to the NYU Club. The club has reciprocal privileges at private and university clubs throughout the United States and the world, as do many other U.S. university clubs. Before leaving to work in the United Kingdom, I got a letter of introduction from the NYU Club to the Oxford-Cambridge Club in London. There is little to compare with having a family or superb club welcome you five thousand miles away from home. Being lonely while traveling on business is to be expected. Even with an overseas family or newfound club friends, don't be surprised at how much you will miss your family and friends.

What about your love and sex life? If you are married, you can go to dinner or a club with your newfound friends, flirt outrageously if you wish, and excuse yourself to call your husband. If the time zones aren't too wildly apart, have a sexy conversation with your husband. If you're single and have a lover back home, you can do the same, but you do have other options as well.

If you are interested in a sexual or romantic encounter, you will have little trouble meeting men who are only too happy to accommodate you. Use the same discretion that you would in New York, Chicago, Atlanta, or Dubuque. As a general rule, avoid clients, colleagues, and men in bars. Try striking up a converstion with a man in a private club, museum, or restaurant, or while sitting at a sidewalk cafe. Even if your foreign-language ability is limited to asking about the daily quotes on pig iron, you will be able to communicate your interest. Many times you will be approached without even trying. Use your judgment. When I was single, I met a man in the Jockey Club restaurant in Madrid after the headwaiter brought me his card on a silver tray. The headwaiter assured me of the man's good character and standing in the Spanish business community. I couldn't help thinking about how much the waiter received in tips for his help, but I decided to be bold. I sent my admirer my business card and told the waiter I'd be delighted to meet him. His English was superb, and I found him to be charming and brilliant, but married. Nonetheless, I enjoyed his company during dinner.

Even during your leisure time, keep your business card with you. If you meet an interesting man, you can offer your card and ask for his. A lot of information appears on those cards, especially in Europe. Some people even list their university degrees after their name! One disarmingly unpretentious man with whom I exchanged cards in London had "O.B.E." after his name indicating that he was an Officer of the Order of the British Empire, a high honor bestowed for exceptional achievements. He was a joy to be with.

Once while working in Bogotá, Colombia, I went up to the rooftop restaurant of the lovely Hotel Tequendama to see the view and look at the menu. I thought I'd make a reservation for the following night, and I asked the maitre d'hotel for a table at 8 o'clock. He asked me in good but accented English if I liked to dance. Thinking he wanted to reserve a place for me at the show that followed dinner, I said yes. When he asked me if I'd care to go dancing with him, I indignantly reminded him that he was the maitre d'hotel and that I had asked for a dinner reservation, not a date. He apologized profusely, but laughed while explaining that he too was a guest at the hotel. He had just arrived from Mexico City, and was using the maitre d'hotel's phone to inquire about his lost luggage! Although I was embarrassed, I apologized and accepted his offer of dinner and dancing. Needless to say, I had a wonderful time.

Spend some time absorbing the culture of the locale. One of the best ways to learn to deal with your clients is to understand their background. Get a good map and walk around. It is interesting to observe the behavior patterns of the people. If you are fortunate enough to be working in a country that has a number of business and professional women in the work force, you may want to see if they have organized into any associations or clubs. A visit with a group of working women will go far toward helping you understand the local business culture.

If you have the time, pretend you are a tourist and absorb the high points of the culture. Visit museums, galleries, shops, and parks, or go to the theater or to a concert. I once spent a day at the Museum of Anthropology in Mexico City and came away with a better understanding of the Mexican personality. On another trip, I spent a few hours in the Museum of Modern Art, also in Mexico City. I was amazed to find a superb retrospective of J.M.V. Turner, the nineteenth-century British painter. Noticing an attractive man, I remarked in Spanish about the light in Turner's works. He turned to me and replied in almost totally unaccented English that, on his recent business trip to New York, his colleagues had teased him about living in a cultural backwater. We exchanged cards and I wasn't a bit surprised to see that Federico Cabrera Rojas was a first vice president of Citibank de Mexico!

If you do meet a man and become emotionally involved with him, what will you do? Do not telex your company and tell them you're never coming back. Seriously though, a long-distance romance is difficult to sustain. Also, it's a good idea to get to know him better than the few days or weeks have allowed. Invite him to visit you the next time he's in the United States, or take your next vacation in his city, and then see how you feel. Most of the time the relationship will not work. But you didn't get this far in business by being either timid or foolish, so if you think it will work, do it!

In some places, such as mainland China, relationships between visitors and locals are discouraged. The Chinese themselves are not sure how close to foreigners they are allowed to get. Chinese businessmen often have to receive permission from their superiors before meeting foreign colleagues for lunch. There are occasionally penalties for those who fail to get an OK. As a foreigner in China, your activities are limited mostly to business and sightseeing.

Of course, you will not be able to socialize with men in most of the Middle East. But if you are so inclined, you can meet and date men in Israel, Egypt, and even Jordan in much the same way as in Western societies.

Whether you are married or single, when you're homesick you can meet people from the United States no matter what country you're in. Most major cities have an American expatriate community where you may even find someone from your home town. Usually the U.S. embassy will be able to give you information on contacting "expats," some of whom have been away for a while and would enjoy a visit from a businesswoman from the United States. Another way to meet Americans is to look up a group like the Brazilian-American or British-

American friendship club. You can find that type of association in many countries. These clubs often sponsor language classes, tours, and social events that are usually of a high quality.

If all else fails and you're still homesick don't forget that McDonalds, Pizza Hut, and Baskin Robbins can now be found around the globe. You can also eat in good U.S.-style restaurants in Paris, London, Tokyo, Madrid, Hong Kong, and even Seoul, Korea. There's a Tokyo outpost of Wolfgang Puck's famous California restaurant, Spago. There is even a replica of Manhattan's Joe Allen steak house in Paris. California nouvelle or Tex-Mex cooking, good burgers, and New England clam chowder can be found in many cities. Don't forget that the American Clubs in Hong Kong, Beijing, Tokyo, Taipei, and Singapore offer excellent food. Check if your own club has a reciprocal arrangement. Having a chili burger and a glass of California Zinfandel in Singapore may not be the same as being in the United States, but it's good to know you can have a little bit of home on the other side of the world.

15

Career, Love, and Family: Having It All

It may be somewhat difficult to breast-feed your baby if you're ten thousand miles away on assignment in Jakarta, Indonesia, but that doesn't mean that you have to choose between your career and your family. One New York woman simply stated to her boss that for six months after the birth of her child she would not be able to travel further than New Jersey. To her delight and surprise, he said: "Are you sure that's all the time you need? I was afraid you wouldn't travel for a year." Granted, not all bosses are that flexible, but don't underestimate your value to the corporation. A good number of employers may be willing to compromise about family situations rather than risk losing you. In fact, when one executive at a large corporation became pregnant, she was promoted to avoid the chance that she would quit.

Smart employers are beginning to realize the need to attract and retain talented employees. In the coming years, the pool of mid-management talent will shrink considerably—a natural consequence of the diminishing baby boom generation. The beneficiaries will be older people who do not want to retire, and women, enough of whom will be in the pipeline to occupy senior management positions.

So, you're in a fairly benevolent corporation, and you have options for advancement, overseas travel, and family. Now, how do you go about having them all? In the past, women who rose high on the corporate ladder didn't have many options. The few executive women in the 1950s through early 1970s often didn't marry or have children. They devoted themselves entirely to their careers. A 1985 poll of 300 executive women showed that 52 percent had either never married, were divorced, or were widowed, and that 61 percent had no children. A 1988 poll of corporate officers taken by Horn/Ferry International showed that 20 percent of the women chief executives never married, while less than 1 percent of the men had never married; according to the same study, over 50 percent of the women were childless, compared with only 5 percent of the men.

Certainly, many of these women were programmed in childhood to believe that being an executive was an unnatural condition for a woman. Today, any combination of roles and lifestyles is acceptable. Even if househusbands are not exactly the norm today, they are no longer the joke they once were.

Young executive women today are advancing further and faster than the women who proceeded them. In the past, most women were not on career tracks that involved travel, because travel was mostly the domain of those executives on the way up. Now, however, women are traveling domestically in record numbers, and traveling overseas with increased frequency. Another recent phenomenon is that male and female executives have begun traveling together. For a while there were complaints, reminiscent of the traditional policemen's wives' complaints about having female recruits in the patrol car. Today that cop's wife is often in the work force too—riding, traveling, or strategizing with men. One woman executive said: "Nobody liked it in the beginning, but now men and women travel together. It's a nonevent."

How can the married executive with children juggle her family, job, and travel? In the best of all possible worlds, she should have a supportive, cooperative husband; a healthy, well-adjusted child; responsible care for the child; an encouraging, understanding boss; and an exciting job. Since this is rarely the case, serious long-term planning is required to manage this kind of juggling act. Most women go to college, and often graduate school, to prepare for a career. A four-year course of study isn't necessary to have a family, but some long-range planning should be part of a woman's preparation if she wants a husband, children, and career.

Of course, you may want just a husband and career, or even just a career. Women today no longer need feel like outcasts for not wanting children or marriage. A psychologist who has studied the differences between women who want children and those who don't says that those who don't are more narcissistic and have high self-esteem, but also have more altruistic goals in their lives. The "will-I-be-lonely-in-my-old-age" argument no longer carries much weight; patterns of aging and families have changed all that. I rarely see my 73-year-old widowed mother, even though she lives only 20 minutes away, because I'm constantly working and she's busy enjoying her recent retirement with her lover.

Because of the U.S. phenomenon of mobility, my hospital-executive sister, who lives in Los Angeles with her husband and son, probably spends more time with my mother. When my mother visits my sister, she usually stays for two to three weeks at a time because, as she aptly puts it, "Traveling to Los Angeles takes almost as long as going to Europe and nobody would stay in Europe for just a few days."

If you do marry a reasonable, caring man (and would you marry any other kind?) you should discuss the choices and options available to you. If you are committed to having children, determine how your husband, boss, and company can work with you to make things easier. The typical corporate child-care policy is light years away from being comprehensive, but these policies aren't standardized, so find out what may be available to you. Some corporations provide child-care facilities, flextime, and/or special financial and other allowance for child care, or will assist you in finding a suitable housekeeper. According to a 1989 survey by Robert Half, "Parent tracks would be a popular option." About 82 percent of women and 74 percent of men said they'd accept slower progress at work in return for more time with family.

Since over 60 percent of all U.S. families (at all levels) are two career couples, and close to 55 percent of women with children work outside the home, it is time for child care to become a part of every company's benefit structure. See what you can negotiate with your employer—you may be pleasantly surprised. Although the United States does not have a national policy of mandated maternity leave, there are efforts underway in Congress to provide tax credits for child care, paid and/or unpaid maternity or paternity leave, and national standards for child care. Some professional women's groups, dissatisfied with the lack of child care available to them, have taken the problem into their own hands. For example, the National Association of Bank Women is mounting a campaign to get financial institutions to provide child care for employees' children.

Women today also have the option of postponing having children until their late 30s if they wish. Many fast-trackers build their reputation over 10 or 12 years and then take some time out for childbearing, often without losing ground in their careers.

If you decide to have a child, try to plan your next full year to your best advantage. Of course, you can travel during most of your pregnancy, although you probably won't want to travel during the last three months. Study your job and plan your schedule as best you can to accommodate both children and career.

While it is hardly a universal trend, younger men seem to be more willing to share home and family responsibilities. Those men who were weaned on Betty Friedan show more initiative in taking care of children, cooking, and nurturing. The majority of men over 45, on the other hand, find it hard to escape the bonds of their traditional upbringing, except for the older men whose consciousness has been raised by their liberated daughters. Men born or raised since the start of the women's movement appear to be more sensitive and flexible than older men.

Most men are willing at least to lend a hand with the housework. If you make enough money, arguments over who does what can be avoided by employing a housekeeper. Otherwise, it might be a good idea to discuss dividing the chores in some fashion. Of course, if you are on the road for a stretch of time, it's somewhat difficult to clean the house or prepare meals. Just as in your international deals, negotiation is always better than confrontation. Involve your husband or partner in finding ways to manage time more effectively.

Things are somewhat easier if you're married or living with someone and don't have children. In this case you only have adult sensibilities with which to concern yourself. There is no question that your time away from home can strain your relationship. What you must do is see your overseas travel as a means to an end—it may help your career take off, or give you the increased earnings to buy a home, or it may give you options for a different kind of career in the future. Eventually, you may be happier getting off the fast track and devoting more time to home, hobbies, or friends. But right now your overseas experience is increasing your options for the future.

What if your husband or partner resents your time away? (You may resent it yourself sometimes.) Here again, you must help him see how your travel will improve your future together. Men are often less verbal and communicative about their feelings, and tend to sulk or become angry about other things instead of discussing the real problem. Ask your husband or partner to help you improve the time you do spend together. Explain that sometimes it's good for couples to be separated for a short time and that separation can refresh a relationship. My husband uses the time that I'm away to catch up on horror movies, neglect the household chores, eat cholesterol-laden food, and go to avant garde jazz concerts. Most of these are things that I don't enjoy and rarely do with him. For both of us it's healthy to occasionally be spared the need to relate to and please each other. And the homecomings are exhilarating and exciting.

Most solid relationships don't break up because one partner is on the road from time to time. But if your relationship is shaky to begin with, traveling can put more strain on it. Success can also strain an already troubled relationship, especially if you make more money than your partner. Some men are unhappy in relationships where they are not the largest breadwinner. Many of them grew up never even knowing a professional woman, much less one who travels internationally and makes a high salary. Talking about it is the best way to overcome these differences.

On the other hand, many men like, or at least don't resent, the fact that their wife travels and earns a lot of money. These men are able to enjoy the perks of your career (not the least of which is a second income). Some companies will give you a day or two in compensatory time if you've been away for a while. Or you can take a few days off before or after your travel to spend time with your husband. If this is not possible, ask him to meet you in London for a long weekend when you're working there, or see if he can take his vacation and accompany you to Rio de Janeiro. My husband thoroughly enjoyed seeing me off to work in Rio each morning while he enjoyed a leisurely breakfast on the hotel terrace. He spent his time swimming, sight-seeing, and drinking *caipirinhas* (Brazilian daquiris) while I spent the day in meetings. Then we would have dinner together and spend a quiet evening in one of Rio's beautiful nightspots. My husband feels good that all the responsibilities are not the sole province of men anymore. He, like many other men today, is secure enough to enjoy the benefits of female careerism.

Another difficult situation is that of the single woman. If you are traveling fairly often, it's not easy to get momentum into a relationship. Relationships need care and nurturing at all times, but the beginning is the most delicate period. If your boyfriend overreacts to your traveling, tell him that you will be thinking of your return during all your waking moments. If either of you uses the short separations as a reason for avoiding the relationship, you are probably not right for each other anyway.

If you're away regularly you may find it difficult even to meet a man. See if you can schedule a fairly long period where you don't travel overseas. August is a good time, as Europe and many other countries are on vacation. Try to take your vacation in a resort near your home town, or go to museums and play tourist at home. Answer or place a personal ad in a reputable publication, or take flying, ballooning, language, or rafting lessons if that's what you've always wanted to do. All the above are fun and will definitely put you in the company of quite a few men.

Women with husbands and children and single women must both adjust to the changes of separation, but the pressures on the single mother may be the most intense. If you are committed to your child and to a job that takes you away from home, quality child care is essential. If you have a parent who is healthy and willing to care for your child while you're away, don't hesitate to ask for help. You may not be sure your parents brought you up in the best way possible, but at least the child will be with your family. If parents or other relatives are unable to care for your child during your trip, make sure you find the best caretakers available outside your family. Start looking far in advance of the trip. It's important that the child (and you) get to know and trust the caretaker. Also, prepare the child for your trip. Explain where you're going and why. Take out maps and show the child where you'll be. Tell the child about the new bike or computer the money you are earning will buy. Most of all, reassure the child that you will return, and give the date. If you are delayed, call the child and explain. If the child is too young to understand, tell him or her anyway. Saying you love the child and that you'll only be in Cairo for two weeks will at least make *you* feel better about the separation.

Another good idea is to tape-record messages for your children before you leave so they will be able to hear your voice whenever they want to. If you're away for an extended period of time, you can also express-mail letters or a tape to them. Ask your husband or friends to tape the children too, and have the tapes sent to you. Calls at regular intervals are important for you and your family. If things are going moderately well at home you will feel much better after a call.

A Note on Relocation

With the focus of business becoming broader and more global, many women today are considering the possibility of relocating, whether to another city in the United States or overseas. While relocating in the United States may be an inconvenience, the problems of becoming an expatriate executive can be enormous. However, so are the rewards. For a single woman with no strong family ties, a stint overseas offers tremendous opportunity with little risk. For a married person with or without children, there is much more to consider before making the decision to relocate overseas.

Some of the problems begin to emerge when a female manager is in line for an overseas assignment. Many corporations believe that even if women are qualified to manage effectively overseas, they will not be accepted as well as men. This is pretty much the same argument used by the senior management (usually male) in resisting women's efforts to travel overseas for short-term business. If you feel that a long-term overseas assignment will benefit your career, make your feelings known.

On the other hand, you must also try to determine your company's long-term plans for you. Although the practice is infrequent, in the past some companies have sent men and women to undesirable posts to get them off the fast track. Today, an overseas assignment often is *the* path *to* the fast track.

If you're offered an overseas assignment, first consider the length of the stay. A six-month assignment is a lot different from a two- to three-year assignment, and involves far less dislocation for you and yours. In a long-term assignment you may have to sell your house or give up or sublet your rental apartment, say goodbye to friends, parents, and all that is familiar, and prepare to immerse yourself in a very different culture and live by its value system. Essentially, you must begin life over. Married women must also take their husband's career and children's schooling into account.

For many people, the change is exhilarating, and a definite growth experience. One banker who felt that New York was constantly becoming dirtier, more dangerous, and more expensive, competitive, and unfriendly, was thrilled to get an offer to relocate herself and her family to Hong Kong. Her husband, an insurance company executive, was able to transfer to a subsidiary of his company in Hong Kong. Since their children were young, three and five years old, it was a relatively easy and agreeable transition for all.

One of the most important factors in relocation is where you're being sent. Adjustment to Western Europe, particularly the major capitals, is fairly easy. However, an assignment to Bangkok, Thailand, is another thing. For some people, the cultural differences may be too much to handle.

If a married couple's relationship is a good one, the stresses of relocation can often be overcome. But don't expect the excitement of a new place to improve a failing marriage. Things can only get worse in a strange country, especially if your husband has trouble finding work or getting a work permit. In some countries he may be breaking the law merely by looking for a job in competition with local workers.

If a position in another country opens up, find out first about the country, and then about your proposed job and what is planned for you when you return to the United States. Your next step is to discuss the move with your family and friends. If, on balance, the position for which you are in line in Tegucigalpa, Honduras, is full of problems for your personal and social life, it may not be worth the anticipated promotion two years later. One woman in such a situation felt that her company was forcing her out with an implied "transfer or leave" attitude. She did leave, but went to another company and a better position.

If you have examined all the considerations and you still feel that relocation is right for you, there are many ways to benefit from the situation. You will undoubtedly become fluent in a foreign language, learn international business practices, and probably be able to travel extensively in the region. You will gain sophistication and a perspective of the world that few people ever have the opportunity to acquire. A stint in a foreign country can be one of the most enriching times of your life.

You will have the most satisfaction from an overseas post if you are energetic, flexible, and strongly motivated, and if you have strong interpersonal skills and a sense of humor. It's easiest to adjust if you are married and your husband is able to work in the country, you are childless or have either very young or grown children, and you are excited by and interested in the country. But not all these factors are prerequisite for success. Even if your husband can't work at his regular job while overseas, he may be able to take a leave of absence from his company and spend the year abroad teaching English or writing the novel he has never had time for. Your relocation may turn out to be the opportunity he has been hoping for.

If you do go, make sure you are going for the right reasons. Wanting to get away from a bad personal or professional situation is usually a poor reason to relocate.

Making sure you are compatible with the culture is almost as important as the nature of your assignment. In fact, they are two sides of the same coin. Don't take an attractive assignment thinking you'll adjust to what you initially feel is an alien culture. You won't. A dynamic single lawyer friend of mine was offered a post in Mexico City. As a third-generation Hispanic-American, she welcomed the opportunity to get closer to her roots. Needless to say, she is thriving, both professionally and personally. On the other hand, a banker acquaintance and "Japanophile" who was hoping for a post in Japan was offered a post in Singapore. She accepted it, thinking she would learn to like it as much as Japan. However, she couldn't adjust to Singapore, and had to return to the United States before her assignment was completed.

Having to return home before your tour is up can be more detrimental to your career than declining the post in the first place. Discuss the assignment with management and find out in what ways the company is prepared to assist your transition from the United States. Some questions you can ask include: Does the company provide language and culture training for you, your husband and children? Will the company assist your husband in obtaining a work permit if he needs it? Could your husband transfer to your company if his skills fit? Could he be assigned overseas as well? What assistance does the company give in finding and paying for housing, household help, schools, accounting, legal and tax advice, medical care, cars and pre- and post-assignment counseling?

Equally important are the questions regarding the job. Knowing how often you will be communicating with the home office and to whom will give you an indication of your position in the hierarchy while overseas. If the post is a possible dumping ground, this is the time to find out, not when you are already overseas. Ask for a written guarantee of a job similar to or a step up from the one you are leaving. The answers you get will tell you what the company plans for your career with them.

You may, if you accept a foreign position, find yourself living at a higher standard than in the United States. Servants are very inexpensive in the developing world, and most middle-class people have at least one or two. The perks of cars, servants, club membership, and a general entree into upper-class status may be hard to let go when you return home. If you are single and find that you have fallen in love with the handsome young local who has been pursuing you for a year, you may find him hard to let go as well. In any case, you can always request another tour of duty from your company. Failing that, and depending on your feelings for the place, you can stay and work for a local company.

The great majority of expatriate executives go home enriched but anxious about the changes they will find. Don't worry, you'll be able to adjust to them and keep on going up the corporate ladder.

16

Women in the World Marketplace: 2000 A.D.

In a 1978 perfume commercial, a woman sang to her husband about her superwoman abilities. In the revised 1984 version of the commercial, she still claimed superwoman status, but asked her husband for a little help occasionally. By the late 1980s, the commercial had been scrapped completely. Soon, hopefully, the superwoman will no longer have to prove herself or ask for help from her husband. He will participate more equally in the housekeeping and child-rearing tasks without having to be asked.

Sociologist Barbara Melber and her Seattle Research Center recently completed a study on male lifestyles in the decades since World War II. She found that men who entered adulthood in the 1950s married early and continue to have stable but traditional marriages. Men of the 1980s generation, on the other hand, live alone longer, marry later, and often divorce and remarry. These men are more involved in household chores, not only because their wives demand it, but because living alone has made them more familiar with the tasks.

As these trends continue, more and more men will be assuming their share of household tasks with genuine interest and enthusiasm. While on the surface women will be the main beneficiaries, in fact men will also benefit in ways of which their fathers never dreamed.

This change is already beginning. Most men today would not be happy to come home to a woman who had spent the day at home as their mothers often did. They seek out women who have stimulating lives. Most men today reject the idea of a relationship with a woman who lives vicariously through her husband. The responsibility of being the strong, silent breadwinner has been overwhelming to most men.

In the future, we will see a blurring of traditional male/female roles. Most important, though, men and women will have options. While many men will continue to function in a fairly traditional fashion, they will also have the opportunity to pursue less traditional lifestyles if they wish. There is already growing acceptance for men who stay home with children full- or part-time. Men can be, and often are, as nurturing as women. It is only their past conditioning that makes some men unemotional.

We are beginning to see new flexibility in love and work relationships. Men and women are taking turns caring for children. It is also no longer unusual for a female attorney to be married to a brilliant, struggling musician, or for a corporate vice president, also female, to be married to a graduate student of anthropology. Nor will it be unheard of for a man to take a break from a career that is no longer satisfying to pursue other options. One study reports that men with working wives are planning earlier retirements than men of previous generations.

In this new equality, everybody wins. I have spoken to a number of young men who are delighted that they are married to or living with high-powered, high-salaried women. They express a sense of relief at not having to assume the financial and emotional burdens alone. Some men expressed embarrassed pleasure at being able to pursue traditionally feminine tasks such as child nurturing, cooking, shopping, and so on. The children are winners too. Men spend more time with children when women work. Children identify more positively with mothers who work. In a 1984 *New York Times Magazine* article, the three-year old daughter of a then-superwoman said she wanted to be a father when she grew up, "because mommies work too hard." However, for most children whose mothers have relatively satisfying careers, a healthy attitude is conveyed to them about combining work and family. One woman wrote recently of spending a weekend with her nine-year-old goddaughter and the goddaughter's best friend. "They reminded me of myself at that age," she wrote, until she asked them what game they were playing. The goddaughter replied: "We're packing our briefcases. We pretend we're going on a business trip."

Women will continue to have more options than ever, both at home and in the workplace. Telecommuting, for example, is a great boon for mothers (and fathers) of very young children. With the spread of fax machines, voice mail, lap-top computers, and other innovations in communications, the whole idea of a single office is changing. It is becoming increasingly possible for an executive to work out of her home, or to go to the central office only during nontraditional hours.

Indeed, many companies no longer even *have* a central office. Modern technology has made it possible to decentralize operations. Citibank, once headquartered solely in New York City, now handles credit cards in North Dakota, clears checks in Delaware, and handles data processing in New Jersey. This trend not only helps companies take advantage of lower rents in suburban areas, it also helps employees work closer to home as companies' operations become more decentralized.

These trends also enable business to function better in a global economy. As one executive recently said, with a fax machine, "I can be in touch with Japan, Africa, Latin America and the U.S.—all in the same day."

While their climb up the corporate ladder hasn't been as fast as most women would like, it is only for the last 15 years at most that substantial numbers of women have worked at managerial levels and above. It will probably take at least another 10 to 15 years before large numbers of women will be at the highest levels of the corporate hierarchy. Already, however, executive women are being sought to fill outside directorships on corporate boards in large numbers.

Change is coming in all sectors of the work force. It is now commonplace to see road signs reading "People Working" instead of "Men Working" at construction sites throughout the United States. Many traditional male preserves are beginning to see women in their ranks.

Women poured into business and professional schools in the 1970s and 1980s, able at last to compete in the careers that were for so long closed to them. While many women are making tremendous inroads in law, business, engineering, and economics, others are dissatisfied with the rate of progress or feel poorly compensated for ten-hour workdays and seven-day workweeks. A fair number of women are leaving those jobs to write, consult, and open their own businesses. One of the most significant changes today is the increase of women-owned businesses. Of the approximately 12,000 new businesses started each week, almost one third are owned by women. These entrepreneurs are involved in every type of venture, including manufacturing, architecture, accounting, and real estate, as well as the traditional women-owned businesses. There are major organizations on the national and local levels, such as the National Association of Women Business Owners, the National Alliance of Home Based Businesswomen (with men making up 10 percent of its membership) and the Women Business Owners of New York, whose memberships are skyrocketing. From 1977 to 1980 alone there was a 33 percent increase in women-owned businesses! During the same period the number of women owned construction companies rose almost 25 percent. If these trends continue, by the year 2000, women will own half the business in the United States. That's progress!

Another aspect of progress is seen in the attitudes of younger women. The *New York Times* recently reported on a Yale student celebrating her 19th birthday at a Manhattan restaurant with her mother, a well-known writer, and a number of other women who are prominent in business, the professions, and politics. Asked if she was impressed by the collective power of the women in the room the student replied, "No, I simply take it for granted."

Since the United States is often an international catalyst for change, we can hope that some of the progress women have made will set an example for change overseas. Gains have been coming elsewhere in the developed world, although slowly. While women have owned small businesses and been in the professions for a long time in Western Europe, they have not yet made much progress in the corporate marketplace, even though they make up 40 percent of the work force. However, two large European banks have recently opened "women's branches" to serve working women in Geneva, Switzerland, and Edinburgh, Scotland. The International Federation of Business and Professional Women has more than 250,000 members.

In the developing world, progress is even slower. Women make up 60 to 80 percent of the agricultural workers in Africa and Asia, and more than 40 percent of those in Latin America. Even here, through their own efforts and those of U.S. businesswomen's associations, many of these women are organizing into cooperatives and communes. They are learning that economic power is personal power.

Some women in the developing world are small-business owners. They are becoming part of a system that will free them from the extreme poverty of many people in their countries. This progress is sure to continue. It is my greatest wish to revise this book in the coming years to read "When in Brazil (or Great Britain, Taiwan, Honduras, Ghana, Italy, etc.) be sure to ask your client for *her* recommendations."

Bibliography

Adler, N. "Women in International Management: Where are They?" *California Management Review*, Summer 1984.

———. "Expecting International Success: Female Managers Overseas." *Columbia Journal of World Business*, Fall 1984.

Cateora, P. *International Marketing*. 5th Ed. Homewood, Il.: Richard Irwin, 1983.

Condon, J. "Foreign Female Executives: Japan's 'Third Gender.' " *Wall Street Journal*, April 2, 1984.

Hill, J. S., and R. R. Still. "Adapting Products to LDC Tastes." *Harvard Business Review*, March–April 1984.

Lanier, A. "Your Manager Abroad: How Welcome, How Prepared?" AMACOM (American Management Association), 1975.

McCormick, Mark. *What They Don't Teach You at Harvard Business School: Notes from a Street-Smart Executive*. New York: Bantam, 1985.

Rossman, M. L. "Japanese Foreign Market Entry Strategies in Latin America." *Baylor Business Studies*, August–October 1982.

———. "The Five Nations of Latin America." *Marketing News* (American Marketing Association), October 11, 1985.

Seligman, S. D. "A Shirtsleeves Guide to Corporate Chinese Etiquette." *The China Business Review*, January–February 1983.

Van Zandt, H. "How to Negotiate in Japan." *Harvard Business Review*, November–December 1970.

About the Author

MARLENE L. ROSSMAN is a consultant, author, and professor who specializes in marketing and international business. Her firm, Rossman, Graham Associates in New York City, also provides sales training and marketing consulting for U.S. and foreign businesses. Ms. Rossman teaches marketing at Pace University Graduate School of Business. She also leads seminars at New York University for women executives on doing business overseas. She has written and lectured on marketing strategies, international trade, and women in business.

Ms. Rossman was born in New York City, where she received a B.A. in English and an M.A. in linguistics from New York University and an M.B.A. in marketing and international business from Pace University. She lives in Manhattan with her husband, Elliot Silverman, a lawyer.